Introduction
to
Bobbin Lacemaking

Introduction
to
Bobbin Lacemaking

REVISED EDITION

Rosemary Shepherd

B.T. Batsford Ltd · London

Acknowledgments

This book would have been inadequate without the encouragement and support of my students, each of whom has contributed by working from the instructions herein. Apart from helping to identify errors, they have also kept me in touch with the special problems of a beginner lacemaker, which are all too easily forgotten when one is more experienced. Some of my students live in remote parts of Australia and learn by correspondence; many have never seen another lacemaker at work. Their determination and enthusiasm are a great inspiration to me.

All photography by Roger Deckker except where otherwise indicated.

Front cover photograph: Roger Deckker
Back cover photograph: Jane Townsend

© Rosemary Shepherd 1983 and 1995

This edition first published in Great Britain in 1996

ISBN 0 7134 7979 5

A CIP record for this book is available from the British Library

All rights reserved. No part of this book may be reproduced in any form or by any means without the permission of the publisher

Printed in Hong Kong for the publisher

B.T. Batsford Ltd
4 Fitzhardinge Street
London W1H 0AH

Contents

Introduction

Bobbin lacemaking is a very old textile craft in which threads wound on small handles or bobbins are twisted and crossed to construct an open and decorative fabric. It can be described as a very free form of weaving in which the warp and weft threads are constantly changing place, a loom of sorts being formed by pins which are pushed into the working surface as the work proceeds to hold the threads in place and assist in tensioning them.

Bobbin lace first appeared in Europe early in the sixteenth century and probably reached its peak of excellence in the late seventeenth and early eighteenth centuries. For almost three hundred years it was a thriving industry, of considerable importance to the economies of many European countries.

The first machine-made laces became available at the end of the eighteenth century. It is popularly supposed that this on its own was responsible for the demise of the hand-made lace industry, but the truth of the matter is far more complicated. For one thing it was only possible to make an acceptable copy of hand-made lace because by this time the artistic merit of such lace had so declined that it was no more than a net with rather insignificant border motifs and 'spots' dotted over the ground. This in turn was the result of the changes in fashion and the demand for very soft trimmings for the simple muslin dresses which were then in vogue. Such simple lace designs were easily embroidered onto the net which was produced by the earliest machines.

Although much exquisite bobbin lace was hand-made for the luxury market during the nineteenth century the industry never again reached the level of demand of earlier centuries. Today some lacemakers in France, Italy, Belgium, Czechoslovakia, Russia and China are able to earn a living from their work but the industry is not a commercial proposition of any significance in any of these regions.

Despite its decline as an industry bobbin lacemaking survives as an art or leisure activity in many countries due largely to new developments this century, especially during the last two decades. In the best contemporary work the maker is also the designer (this was never the case in earlier times) and although much new work is still designed within the traditional framework, a strong group of lacemakers is emerging whose work is regarded more as art in that it goes beyond technique; technique is pushed to its limits in the service of the idea. Whatever their particular interest the possibilities for today's lacemakers are far more exciting and satisfying than they ever were for the professional lacemakers of pre-industrial Europe.

Because it requires considerable application, bobbin lacemaking is a wonderfully effective relaxation. The basic movements and stitches are few and quickly learned, but their application could fill a lifetime of happy hours and still leave many ways of working unexplored. Many lacemakers today are happy mastering the skills of traditional lacemaking, and working only on the designs they find in the excellent books now available. For all lacemakers this must be the starting point, but the future strength of the craft depends on those who accept the challenge of applying the traditional techniques to their own designs, and of finding new ways of working, as well as new uses for the work, which might be more appropriate for our time.

About This Book

This book was written in an attempt to fill a gap in the existing literature on the subject by providing a detailed and thorough introduction to the basic skills of bobbin lacemaking without involving the reader too heavily in any particular lacemaking tradition. One's early experience of any craft is important in determining future enjoyment, but for an intricate craft like lacemaking a confident and adequately informed start is quite essential.

The book is intended not only for those who wish to teach themselves but also for the use of teachers in schools and colleges who would like to include bobbin lacemaking in their textile arts programmes. The coloured projects in particular were designed with young people in mind, and the book also contains instructions for making the basic equipment simply and cheaply.

The need for such an elementary book is particularly Australian. There can be few countries where people are so dependent on the written word for instruction in all kinds of craft activity. The availability of classes is improving for many crafts, but it will be a long time before there are enough classes in bobbin lacemaking to meet the demand. For that reason the scope of the book is limited, in the interests of being thorough and unambiguous at the basic level, to an extent which is just not necessary in most other countries where lacemaking has been established longer. Many excellent books have come from these countries over the last decade, but most assume more familiarity with the craft than exists here. I hope that this volume will give its Australian readers the background and confidence to make better use of the imported books.

Unfortunately, there are almost as many different ways of describing the basic stitches as there are books on the subject, and I have not been able to find a way around this. I can only hope that after working through this book the new lacemaker will have sufficient understanding to follow the photographs and diagrams in other books when the verbal description seems confusing. In fact, the terms 'cross' and 'twist' appear in most books; it is only the names for the stitches they are combined in which vary. Once the sequence of movements in a stitch can be identified its name is not so important.

How To Use The Book

There are two main categories of bobbin lace: continuous laces, in which pattern and background are worked at the one time, and sectional laces, in which the separate parts of a design are completed before being joined together by the mesh background. In working a design for continuous lace the number of bobbins is directly dependent upon the width of the lace; in some of the very fine old laces several hundred bobbins were often used at one time. Sectional laces, on the other hand, seldom use more than twenty-four bobbins, as each motif is generally built up from a narrow braid. Some famous continuous laces are Valenciennes, Lille, Bedfordshire and Buckinghamshire Point, and the most famous sectional laces are probably Brussels and Honiton.

This book contains exercises in modern Torchon lace, a continuous lace, the techniques of which are easily applied to other kinds of lacemaking. Torchon lace is logical, flexible, and comparatively easily understood. Properly learned it also establishes good working habits which will simplify the progression to more complex laces.

If you have never before attempted bobbin lacemaking you would be wise to work your way methodically through the book in the order it is written, although it is only necessary to work one of the exercises from each of Chapters 4, 6 and 12. If you are a very young person seek the help of a parent or teacher with anything that seems hard to understand. If you have had some experience of Torchon, or one of the other continuous laces, it would still be sensible to work the basic sampler in Chapter 3 before moving on to the more advanced exercises.

The patterns for the exercises are all on a rather large scale so that you can see easily what is happening to the threads as you work. It would be simplest just to trace or photocopy these from the pattern diagrams, but I recommend you take the extra trouble to copy the pattern diagram on to your own graph paper, following the relevant pattern construction notes. This may seem tedious but you will appreciate the discipline when later you come to design your own patterns, or to reduce the given patterns for use with finer thread. You will also find it a great help in understanding the structure of your lace; you will never have quite the same understanding if you only trace or photocopy the patterns.

Finally, I suggest that you read through each chapter before you begin working on it, then read it again as you are working. Do not be tempted to launch into the exercises using only the diagrams and photographs (although this may sometimes be possible) as there are important details in the text which you may miss, thus limiting your grasp of later exercises. The first chapters are rather wordy as it is important that you gain a thorough understanding of the basic elements of the craft. However, if a particular process still seems unclear to you, do not agonise over it; move on to the next section and you will probably find that the problem is easily solved when you return to it later. Do not be afraid of mistakes either, or worry unduly if your first efforts are not up to the standard of the samples in the photographs. As long as you understand what you are doing, proceed to the next exercise and you will find that your work will improve with practice.

Configuration of the Diagrams

In the earliest exercises, where every small detail is important, each diagram is fully representational in that it shows the threads exactly as they would appear in an enlargement of the lace. In later exercises I have sometimes taken shortcuts by drawing the threads passing through each other, instead of over and under as would in fact be the case. If you are ever in doubt about the configuration of a particular diagram refer to the diagrams below.

Bobbins', 'pairs' and 'threads'
Throughout the book the phrases 'pairs of bobbins', 'pairs of threads', or just 'pairs' are used synonymously.

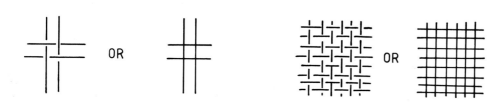

Diagram 1 *Cloth stitch; also known as whole or linen stitch*

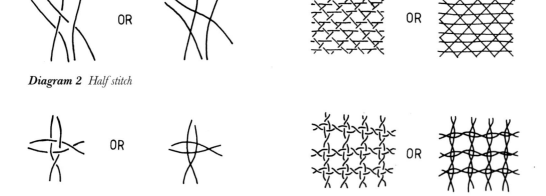

Diagram 2 *Half stitch*

Diagram 3 *Cloth-stitch-and-twist, generally abbreviated to cloth-and-twist; also known as double half stitch or whole-stitch-and-twist, and sometimes double stitch*[1]

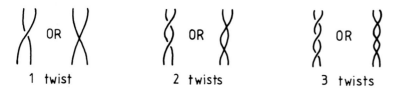

1 twist   2 twists   3 twists

Diagram 4 *One pair twisted*

---

[1] European and some American lacemakers work half stitch *twist + cross* instead of *cross + twist*. Their whole stitch then very logically becomes two of these, that is, *twist + cross + twist + cross*. This is the same as cloth-and-twist, excepting that the movements are reversed. The finished lace will be the same, regardless of the order in which the movements are made.

1 Equipment and Materials

There are a number of specialist suppliers of lacemaking equipment and materials whose names are listed at the back of the book, and most are happy to supply mail orders. The total cost of all the requirements listed, excluding the work table and light, is about $150 at the present time (1995). However, the list includes some small items you are likely to have already, and it is quite possible to make for yourself the most expensive items, namely the pillow and the bobbins.

The Lace Pillow

(Some kinds of needle lace are also made on a pillow, the shape and use of which is quite different from that of a bobbin lace pillow.)

The lace pillow is the surface upon which the lace is made, the lace threads being woven and plaited around pins which are pushed into the pillow as the work proceeds to hold the lace in shape. The pillow needs to be firm enough to hold the pins upright when the lacemaker is tensioning the threads, but not so firm that great effort is required to insert the pins.

The term 'pillow' for this most important piece of equipment probably comes from the early days of bobbin lacemaking when the lace pillow not only resembled either a flat or bolster-shaped bed pillow, but was possibly also stuffed with the same material, namely straw or horsehair. Few of us nowadays would choose to lay our heads upon such a pillow, but many experienced lacemakers still prefer to work on a straw-filled lace pillow, whatever the modern alternatives.

There are many different kinds of lace pillow in use around the world today, and some of them are very elaborate and versatile. The exercises in this book, however, are best worked on a standard 45 cm (18") round or square pillow which is mushroom-shaped in cross section. The slightly curved surface of such a pillow allows the bobbins to fall away from the work, thus keeping the threads taut and helping the tension of the lace. Several suppliers sell this basic kind of pillow, but it is best to inquire about construction as some are straw-filled and others are made of high-density polystyrene foam. The latter may not stand up to constant pricking particularly well, but have the advantage of being very light.

Temporary Lace Pillows

For those who wish to make a lace pillow, instructions are given below. The method given has been thoroughly tried and tested and uses materials which should be readily available.

If you have not the time to make a pillow, and do not want to buy one, an adequate temporary pillow can be made from a 45 cm (18") square of caneite (the material from which pin-boards are often made) covered with plain-coloured cloth, or even brown paper. A slightly more robust board could be made for use in schools by gluing together a piece of caneite and a piece of masonite or pine board, and slipping the resultant sandwich into a washable cloth bag. Either kind of board needs to be used on a sloping surface, or to have some slope built into it by fixing under its back edge a piece of timber or thick foam rubber. A board is only suitable for working straight pieces, in fairly coarse thread; fine lace needs fine pins which are hard to push into the caneite without their bending.

Making a Standard Lace Pillow

It is much easier and less wasteful of materials to make a square pillow than a round one. On the other hand many people prefer to work on a round pillow. For whichever you decide upon you will need the following items.

1. A 45 cm (18") square or circle of 1 cm (³/₈") particle board for the baseboard.
2. A piece of jute carpet underlay, or several layers of old towelling or blanket, the same size as the baseboard.
3. One metre (1 yd) of heavy unbleached or bleached calico, at least one metre (1 yd) wide.
4. About 3 kg (7 lbs) of clean straw, which is generally obtainable by the bag from pet shops, garden suppliers, produce merchants or farmers. Remove the nodes from the straw and pick out any grain still on the stalks, then cut what remains into pieces roughly 15 cm (6") long. If you cannot get straw, chaff, hay, woodwool or coconut fibre are all acceptable substitutes; it is even possible to use shredded paper if you are careful to pack it into the pillow very tightly.
5. Heavy linen carpet thread or heavy nylon fishing line.
6. A large needle.
7. A large crochet hook.

8. Heavy sewing machine thread for the preliminary sewing.

From the calico cut four pieces, a bare 2 cm (³/₄") bigger all around than the baseboard. Seam the four pieces together with a 1 cm (³/₈") seam, leaving one side of the square unstitched for a square pillow, or almost half of the circumference for a circular pillow. Turn the resulting double-sided bag right side out. Lay the bag on a table and insert the baseboard between the two bottom layers and the underfelt between the two top layers, then close these two pockets separately using the zipper foot on your machine (a somewhat tricky manoeuvre which could be done by hand if you prefer).

You now have a square (or round) bag composed of two sealed calico pockets, seamed together, one enclosing the baseboard and the other enclosing the underfelt. If you are making a round pillow you will need to continue the main seam so that only a 20 cm (8") opening remains. Now stuff straw into the bag, ramming it down very hard, a little at a time, with a length of dowelling or a wooden spoon. It is a good idea to use rubber gloves when packing in the straw. This is the most tiresome part of the whole procedure, and it takes time to achieve a smooth, hard, evenly padded pillow. Keep packing in the straw and compressing it until it protrudes about 3 cm (1¼") above the opening.

Now thread the needle with 3 metres (3¼ yds) of carpet thread, doubled and knotted to make a sewing length of one and a half metres. Holding the pillow between your knees, make large oversewing stitches about 2 cm (³/₄") apart, catching one side of the pillow opening to the other, over the protruding straw. Now pass the needle and thread into your left hand, and ease the two edges of the opening together by progressively tightening each stitch with the

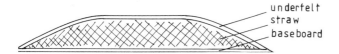

underfelt
straw
baseboard

Diagram 1.1 *Cross section of the lace pillow*

crochet hook, held in your right hand. Pull the excess thread through with your left hand. Be careful not to pull up too much at a time lest you split the cloth. When both edges are together you should have enough thread free to oversew tightly back to the other end, over the first stitches, to finish off.

As a final touch, to compact the straw and smooth out any remaining bumps, turn the pillow upside-down on the floor and 'walk' on its baseboard. Anyone watching this will be quite convinced that you are mad, but you will have a very good lace pillow by way of consolation!

The Pillow Cover and Working Cloths

Your pillow also needs a washable cover made from a smooth plain fabric such as headcloth, in a dark colour. For a square pillow, make a bag to fit the pillow as smoothly as possible, with tape ties to close it. For a round pillow cut a circle of fabric 60 cm (24") in diameter. Face the edge with bias binding to make a casing for elastic of just sufficient length to keep the cover stretched smoothly over the pillow.

From the same fabric make two small cloths, each about

Plate 1.2 *Closing the pillow opening*

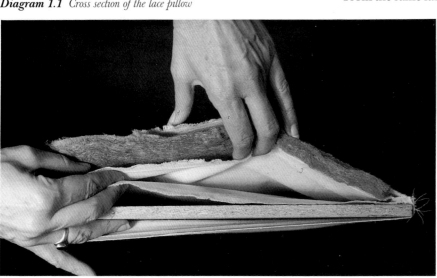

Plate 1.1 *Underfelt and baseboard inserted in calico pockets*

30 cm by 45 cm (12" x 18"); one cloth will go under the bobbins with which you are working, and the other will cover the completed work to keep it clean. The latter is, of course, hardly necessary for the beginning exercises, but will be important when you are making a long length of lace. It is also important to cover the whole pillow when you are not working, with another larger cloth such a tea towel, a small table cloth, or even a square head scarf.

Bobbins

The lace bobbins serve three purposes; they store the thread for the lace, they act as handles by which the threads are manipulated to make the lace, and they weight the threads to keep them tensioned against the pins. There are a number of different bobbins available from the suppliers listed and they vary greatly in price from simple mass-produced wood or plastic bobbins to beautiful hand-turned bobbins which are almost collectors' items. You will use only 14 bobbins for the first exercise, but you need up to 44 bobbins to complete all the projects in the book, so it is sensible to buy the cheaper bobbins at this stage.

Most of those currently available in the lower price range are the light English-style bobbins, which need weighting, or 'spangling', with beads to stop them rolling about too much as you work and to assist with tensioning the threads. For spangling you will need the following items:

1. About 5 metres (5$\frac{1}{2}$ yards) of 30 gauge copper or brass wire, or 15 amp fuse wire.
2. A pair of long-nosed pliers.

3. A pair of wire cutters or an old pair of scissors.
4. Enough glass or china beads to put 5 or 7 on each bobbin. If you have no old necklaces to take apart, inquire at your local opportunity shop before buying new beads, as such places often have broken necklaces which they are happy to sell for a few cents.

For each bobbin cut 8 cm (3") of wire; pass one end of the wire through the hole in the end of the bobbin and thread the beads on to the other end. Twist the ends of the wire together with the pliers to make a closed loop, and finish by cutting off the excess wire and turning the cut ends under so that they do not catch on the thread or on other bobbins.

Many people make their own bobbins, and enjoy finding ingenious methods which do not involve wood-turning. It is actually quite simple to whittle bobbins from 6 mm or 1 cm ($\frac{1}{4}$" or $\frac{3}{8}$") dowelling, or even from straight twigs, cut into 11 cm (4$\frac{1}{2}$") lengths; a neck to hold the thread is then gradually cut away, about 0.5 cm ($\frac{1}{4}$") from one end and about 3 cm (1$\frac{1}{4}$") long.

An even simpler kind of bobbin can be made from meat skewers, which are cut from hardwood dowel and are therefore denser and heavier than standard ramin dowel. Cut the end off a skewer to give a length of 13 cm (5"). Then 0.75 cm (about $\frac{1}{4}$") from one end make a groove all around the skewer with a hacksaw, being careful not to saw too deeply. Now take a sharp knife and cut away the wood from the lower edge of the groove to give a shape like that of the bottom bobbin in the diagram. The disadvantage of this kind of bobbin is that one's hands are more likely to touch the thread since there is no recessed neck upon which to wind it, but in every other respect it works well and would be ideal for use in schools.

All three kinds of whittled bobbins need to be thoroughly smoothed with sandpaper before use, or the thread will catch on them and become fluffy. The fine dowelling bobbins also need to be spangled, but those made of 1 cm ($\frac{3}{8}$") dowel or meat skewers are heavy enough without beads.

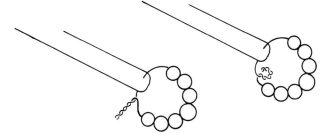

Diagram 1.2 *Spangling the bobbins*

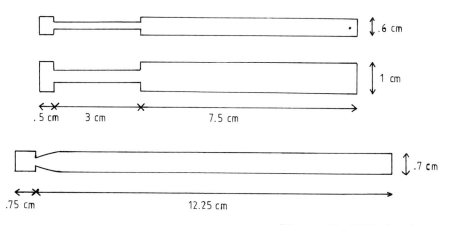

Diagram 1.3 *Bobbin dimensions*

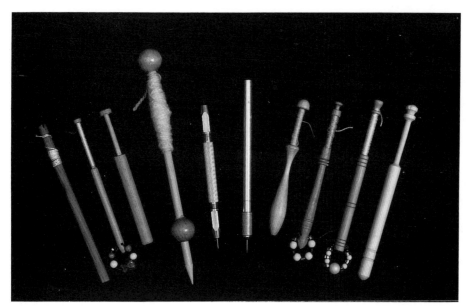

Plate 1.3 *Bobbins of various kinds, and two prickers. The four bobbins on the left are home-made*

Thread

To complete all the exercises in the book you will need to purchase several different thicknesses of thread.

For the beginner exercises in Chapters 3 to 8 inclusive choose from the following threads:

1. Linen lacemaking thread, size 35/2 or 40/2. The Swedish Bockens 35/2 is available in a range of colours as well as white, cream and ecru, and comes wound on a reel of about 200 metres (220 yds) length.
2. Cotton perle no 12. DMC brand is available in a small range of colours as well as white and cream but the colours are sometimes in short supply. Each ball of this thread is 129 metres (140 yds) long.
3. Any other thread of equivalent thickness.

Whichever thread you choose you will need about 200 metres (220 yds) of a pale main colour, and smaller quantities of three medium-toned contrasting colours. For the early exercises it is quite all right to mix cotton and linen in the one piece. In fact if both kinds of thread are available I suggest you buy one reel of linen for your main colour and three balls of perle cotton for the contrast, as this would be cheaper than purchasing all linen.

For the exercises in Chapters 9 to 19 choose from the following threads:

50/2 or 60/2 linen lacemaking thread.

Madeira Tanne cotton, no 12.

Any other yarn of equivalent thickness to the above.

A hank of cotton perle no 5, or equivalent, for use as a gimp (outlining) thread as required.

For Chapter 20 you will need a reel of 30/2 or 50/3 linen to work the collars to the same scale as the originals, but patterns are also given for working both collars in 35/2 or 40/2 linen.

Linen and cotton lacemaking threads are available only from the specialist suppliers listed at the end of the book, but perle cotton is often available in craft or embroidery shops. The linen thread currently available in this country is imported from Sweden, Belgium or Ireland. Both Swedish and Irish linens come on small reels so the initial outlay is less, but the large cones of Belgian thread are a more economical buy.

When buying linen thread always check the size carefully. The larger of the two numbers refers to the size of the separate component threads of the yarn and the smaller number indicates how many threads of that size have been twisted together to make the finished yarn. Thread marked 35/3 will therefore be thicker than that marked 35/2.

Pins

Rustless pins are essential for lacemaking, to avoid having rust marks on your lace. Medium-sized brass or stainless steel pins are the most suitable for working the exercises to the given scale but you will need the finer size for reductions of the patterns.

Brass pins are usually only available from specialist suppliers, but stainless steel pins are generally available, in several sizes, from good haberdashery departments. In my opinion stainless steel pins are superior to brass because they do not discolour and they do not bend. If you improvise with ordinary dressmaking pins do not leave them too long in your pillow as they rust very quickly, despite the fact that they claim to be rustless. In my experience only pins marked 'stainless steel' are truly rustless.

Graph Paper

You will need a generous quantity of both 8 to the inch (3 mm) and 10 to the inch (2.5 mm) graph paper to make the patterns to the given scale. These graph papers are generally available on special order from good stationers, or you may photocopy the sheets at the back of the book.

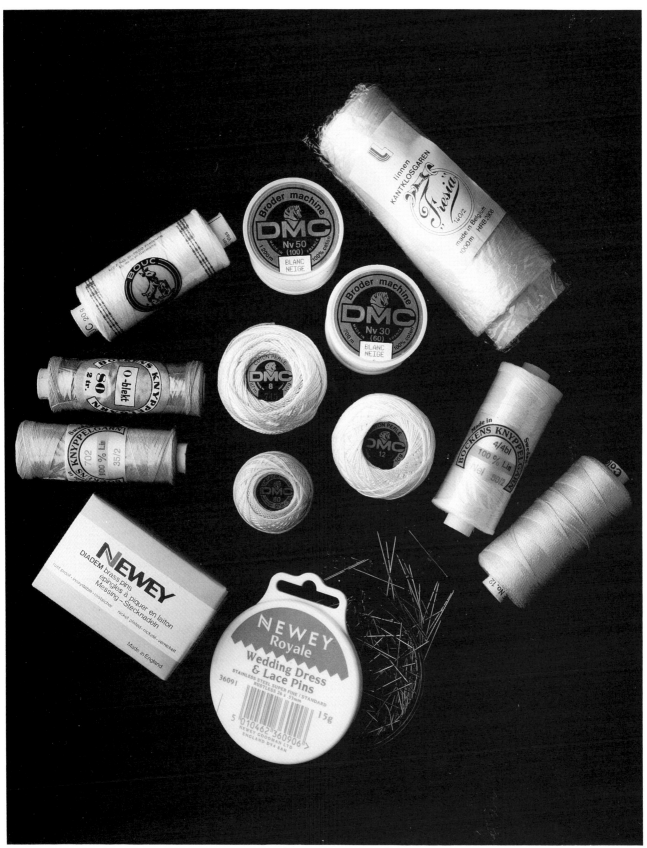

Plate 1.4 *Some of the different threads suitable for lacemaking (photograph Sue Stafford)*

Try to copy them blue or green as black is very hard to work on.

You will also need a few sheets of 2 mm and 2.5 mm (10 to the inch) polar graph paper, and a similar quantity of ordinary 2 mm graph paper.

Pricking Card

The working pattern of traditional bobbin lace is known as a pricking. Originally prickings were made from parchment and many have survived a century or so to be used by today's lacemakers. Today a pricking consists of a piece of thin glazed cardboard with the pattern of pin holes pricked through it according to a pre-planned design. For Torchon lace the design is worked out first on graph paper. The pins which secure the stitches of the lace are pushed through the holes of the pricking into the pillow as you work. To prevent irregularities in the lace it is therefore important that the pricking is accurate and that the pricking card is strong enough not to tear when you tension the threads against the pins. For the sake of your eyes the card needs also to be of a restful colour which contrasts with the colour of your thread. For the first exercises you can improvise with the unprinted surface of a cereal packet, the back of a writing pad, or even with several layers of heavy brown paper, glued together.

Pricker

As a temporary measure you may use a hat pin or bead-headed pin to make your prickings but these are uncomfortable for prolonged use. A very adequate pricker may be made by drilling a hole in the end of a piece of dowelling and gluing a no. 6 needle into the hole with a suitable strong adhesive. Alternatively, you can purchase the kind of inexpensive craft knife which has a slim tubular handle and a collar tightening device, and substitute for its blade a short no. 6 needle. A no. 6 needle seems suitable for most work. If the needle is too small, you will have difficulty pushing the pins into the holes it makes in the pricking; brass pins in particular would then be likely to bend. On the other hand, if the needle is too large the pins will move about in the holes it makes and the lace will not be accurate.

Pricking Mat

When you are making a pricking you need a firm, flat, porous surface under the pricking card to receive the needle point. A cork mat or a piece of caneite suits the purpose well.

Clear Plastic Film

In the past it has been customary to remove the graph paper pattern once the card has been pricked, and to copy the pattern markings onto the card.

There were two reasons for this duplication; one was to avoid the confusion of working with white thread on white paper, and the other was to avoid the misalignment of holes which might occur when the two layers (paper and card) were curved over the lace pillow. The latter is probably not a serious possibility on the kind of pillow described in this book as its working surface is only slightly curved, and the former problem may now be overcome by the simple expedient of covering the graph paper with transparent tinted adhesive film which is available in a range of colours. The clear untinted film is suitable for use with coloured thread. If you can, find a film which has a matt surface.

Equipment for Drawing Up Patterns

♦ Ruler, pencil, compass or circle template and rubber.
♦ Pen and ink.

If you wish to work on the card pricking in the traditional manner it is essential to mark it with waterproof drawing ink, not with felt pen which may mark the lace. Fine felt pen markings may of course be used with safety under plastic film.

Needlework Equipment

♦ 0.6 mm crochet hook for joining up and taking 'sewings'.
♦ Small pair of sharp scissors.
♦ Crewel needles of varying sizes for finishing off and mounting.

Work Table

It is very important to have your pillow supported at a comfortable height and angle while you work if you are to avoid straining your neck and shoulder muscles. You will probably find an ordinary dining table too high and too flat, but if you sit back from it a little and support the back edge of your pillow on the table and its front edge on your lap you should be reasonably comfortable. As you work down the pillow and the bobbins start to hang in your lap you can slide the pillow right on to the table. If this arrangement does not work for you, and you do not have a lower table such as a card table or a typing table, you might consider making or buying a folding pillow stand, or one of those small tables on castors which is adjustable for both height and slope.

Light

I am sure I will be accused of stating the obvious in including light amongst the requirements for lacemaking. Of course no-one will try to work in the dark, but it is my experience that many try to work with inadequate light, especially at night. If you are not working in daylight, try to work in a room with good general illumination, as well as a lamp which can be directed right at your pillow.

2 Preparing to Work

Making a Pricking

The first stage in making a pricking for any piece of lace is to work out the design on paper. For Torchon and other geometric laces it is convenient to use graph paper. Take a sheet of the size of graph specified and mark it exactly as shown in the relevant pattern diagram. Dots always mark the position of pin holes, and a zigzag line generally indicates the passage of worker threads. Other markings will be explained as they arise. When you are sure that all your markings are correct go over them with a fine felt pen or drawing ink so that they are clearly visible. It is advisable to make this and all other insertion or edging prickings 20 cm (8") long . This is the optimum workable length for the size of pillow you have been recommended to use, and will enable you to make a sample of worthwhile size. If you are also careful to use durable card you will be building up a library of prickings for future use; it is a waste of the considerable time and effort involved in its preparation if a pricking is only useable once.

If you are using a caneite board you can work straight onto the graph paper pattern without the under layer of card, although you would be wise to cover the paper with adhesive plastic film so that the ink markings do not come off on your lace.

If you are to work on a pillow you will need to make a pricking* as follows:

Cut a piece of pricking card 1 cm (³/₈") bigger all around than the paper pattern. Position the graph paper pattern centrally on the card and hold it in place temporarily with a small piece of sticky tape top and bottom. Then cut a piece of clear plastic film the same size as the card and stick it over both paper and card so that all three are fastened firmly and smoothly together. Now place this 'sandwich' on your pricking mat and prick through it at all the dots marked on the graph paper. (Do not be tempted to short-cut this procedure by pricking as you work; that will not save time, nor will it be accurate. And, as well, you may bend the pins.) The pricking is now ready for use and should be pinned through its corners to the middle of the lace pillow, and as far towards the top of the pillow as its edge slope will allow. Finally, pin a working cloth over both pricking and pillow, leaving the top 7 or 8 cm (3") of the pricking exposed. (A square or round pricking must be pinned to the centre of the pillow.)

In my opinion new lacemakers learn a great deal about the structure and design of lace by working over the graph paper. However, I know some lacemakers find the graph paper lines a hindrance rather than a help. If you come to feel this way simply revert to the traditional method of making a pricking, which is to remove the graph paper pattern when the holes are pricked and to copy the working markings on to the card.

Winding the Bobbins

For simplicity the diagrams show bobbins wound clockwise only. To do this, first tie the thread end to the neck of the bobbin with a single overhand knot, then, holding the bobbin in your left hand, wind away from you with your right hand, tightly and evenly. (If you are left-handed hold the bobbin in your right hand and wind towards you with your left hand.)

Because the lace bobbins (or more correctly, the lace threads) are always used in pairs we never speak of them in the singular. When starting new work the pairs of bobbins are always 'coupled'—that is, wound from opposite ends of the one length of thread. The simplest way to do this without tangling the thread is to fill completely one bobbin of a pair from the ball of thread, then wind half the thread from the first bobbin on to the other bobbin of the pair. You should have about 25 cm (10") of free thread between the two bobbins when you have finished winding.

To prevent the thread from unwinding as you work, hitch it around the neck of the bobbin as shown in diagram 2.1. This is not always as simple as it seems, so check each stage carefully and make sure that your bobbins are all wound clockwise to start with.

To release more thread whilst you are working, simply turn the bobbin at right angles to the thread and roll it towards you. To shorten the thread lift the loop on the hitch with a pin and roll the bobbin away from you (diagram 2.2).

---

* In this book the term pricking will always refer only to the actual working pattern pricked in card. Some lacemaking books also refer to the graph paper pattern, or pattern diagram, as a pricking.

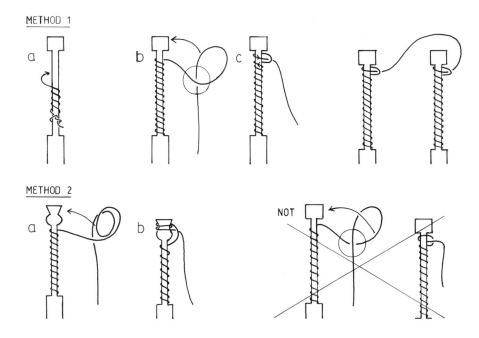

Diagram 2.1 *Hitching the thread on a bobbin*

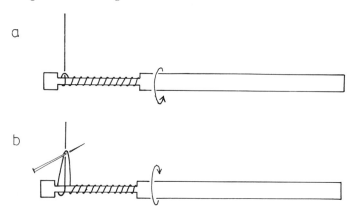

Diagram 2.2 *(a) Releasing thread from a bobbin. (b) Shortening the thread*

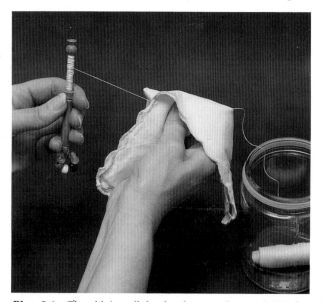
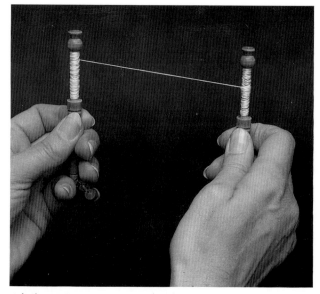

Plate 2.1 *Thread being rolled rather than wound on to a bobbin from the reel (left), and from another bobbin (right)*

Another method of winding the bobbins is as follows: unwind enough thread from the ball for one bobbin, say 3 metres (3¼ yds), and without cutting the thread wind the first bobbin up to the ball; unwind another 3 metres (3¼ yds), cut the thread, and wind the second bobbin from this cut end to within 25 cm (10") of the first bobbin.

Further Notes on Bobbin Winding

The method of winding bobbins just described is quite adequate for your first exercises, but when you are more advanced in your lacemaking, particular thought should be given to the following points.

The twist on the thread you are using

If you roll the bobbin rather than wind the thread (there is a difference), either by hand or with a bobbin winder, you will avoid interfering with the twist in the thread. This is a most important consideration when using the finer threads which might easily un-ply and break (plate 2.1).

Keeping the thread clean

When you are winding a bobbin directly from the reel of thread, apply the necessary tension to the thread with your fingers, through a clean white handkerchief. It will also help if you place the reel of thread inside a jar or bowl so that it cannot roll away from you whilst you are winding.

Clockwise and anti-clockwise

When you read other lacemaking books you will discover that there are national differences in the direction of winding bobbins. European lacemakers wind their bobbins anti-clockwise, whereas in English speaking countries they are generally wound clockwise. Historically this may have arisen from the twist in the thread used in the different countries; thread with a right hand (S) twist would have been wound anti-clockwise and left hand (Z) twisted thread clockwise, so that the twist was enhanced rather than un-done. Whatever the reason for the difference it is quite clear that the direction of winding bobbins has no effect whatever upon the actual lacemaking process. What does matter, however, is that you are consistent so that the direction of winding, hitching and unwinding all become automatic and therefore faster. For simplicity all diagrams in this book show bobbins wound clockwise.

Useful Tips For Later

The following hints will not mean much to you at this stage, but read them anyway so that you will know where to refer when the need arises.

Position of the Hands

When you begin lacemaking, you will probably move the bobbins on the pillow to make the stitches, but as you become more confident you may feel more comfortable and more in control if you hold the pairs one in each hand as you work the stitches. Many lacemakers work in this way, but by no means all of them. Which method you choose is for you to decide, but it would be wise to cultivate some flexibility in the matter; with very fine thread and small bobbins, for example, it may be easier and better for the thread to work on the pillow.

Broken Threads, or Threads Running Out

If a thread breaks close to the work, undo enough stitches so that about 1 cm (³⁄₈") of the broken thread is free; now tie the end of the thread still on the bobbin to a pin well back in the lace, and lay the bobbin down in its original place, ready to work on. When you have finished, darn in the long end for 1 or 2 cm (about ½").

To deal with a broken thread some distance from the work, or to add extra thread, simply knot the ends together with a weavers' knot, which if properly made may have its ends trimmed very short without danger of its coming undone (diagram 2.3). For the first samples only, the knot may be worked into the lace, but for later work it should be dealt with by passing the section of thread with the knot in it around a pin further back in the lace, then laying the bobbin

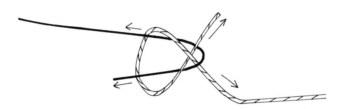

Diagram 2.3 *A weaver's knot*

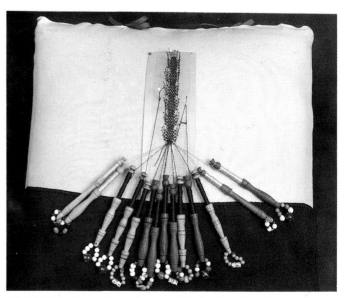

Plate 2.2 *Dealing with a broken thread (left) and passing a knot away (right)*

down in its original place before working on. The knot is later cut away and the ends darned in (diagram 2.4).

If you find that a bobbin is running out of thread, take a full bobbin and fasten it to the almost empty bobbin with a rubber band, having secured its free end to a pin as previously described. Work the two bobbins together for about 2 cm (3/4"), then remove the rubber band and lay the empty bobbin back over the work to be cut off later.

Making a Faulty Stitch

After the first exercises, when you are no longer using contrast threads in strategic places, it is best to avoid having to cope with a join or knot in a worker thread within an area of whole or cloth stitch. Instead, make a faulty stitch near a pin where it will not be noticed so that the knotted thread, or thread which is running out, is exchanged for a passive thread which will carry on as a worker. The offending thread may then be dealt with by one of the methods previously described and the resultant join will be far less conspicuous than a join in a worker thread. Some lacemakers prefer to avoid any kind of join in half stitch, and this is quite possible if you plan ahead and exchange threads in the ground so that any thread which may need a join does not enter the half stitch area.

Just how you make the faulty stitch will depend on the position of the offending thread, but it will generally involve making an extra twist within the stitch before the pin. Diagram 2.4 shows how this is done.

Plate 2.3 '*Moving up*'; *bobbins supported in the working cloth bag*

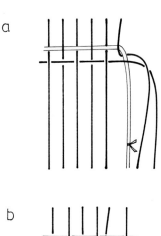

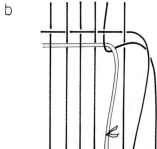

Diagram 2.4 *A method of making a faulty whole stitch to exchange a worker thread for a passive thread: (a) when the knot is in the right hand worker thread and (b) when the knot is in the left hand worker thread*

'Moving Up'

If you wish to work a longer piece of lace than your pricking or pillow allows you must move the work and bobbins up the pillow so that you can start at the top of the pricking again. To do this, first fold your working cloth over the bobbins to make a bag; now slide the bag up the pillow until all the threads between the bobbins and the work have slackened, and pin the bag to the pillow so that it continues to support the full weight of the bobbins (plate 2.3). It is now safe to remove all the pins from the lace so that you can move both it and the bag of bobbins far enough up the pillow to be able to re-pin the last 5 cm (2") of lace worked, into the top 5 cm (2") of the pricking, with the bag still supporting the bobbins. This done, release the bobbins and continue working.

Calculating the Amount of Thread Required

Bobbin lace does not use a great deal of thread; in fact most threads only need to be about three times the length of the finished lace, unless they are worker threads. In some instances I have indicated how much thread to wind on each bobbin, but generally speaking, if you are going to make a useful length of lace, or a number of samples in similar thread, it is sensible to wind all bobbins fully and equalise their use by making the occasional faulty stitch to exchange a worker for a passive or ground stitch thread. When a pattern requires the bobbins to be coupled at the start (see notes on bobbin winding) and you have separate bobbins cut from a previous exercise with plenty of thread remaining, these bobbins may be knotted together in pairs, and the knot wound well on to one or the other so that it will not interfere with the starting procedures. If you are only working a small sample it is possible to wind all the knots far enough on to avoid encountering them; for a longer piece wind the knots on so that they will emerge in different places, to be dealt with as previously described.

3 The Basic Movements and Stitches

Materials:
35/2 or 40/2 linen or no. 12 cotton perle or equivalent
3 mm (8 to the inch) graph paper

In a piece of Torchon lace (or any other continuous lace for that matter) there are usually three main elements, namely, the mesh background, the open pattern areas and the solid pattern areas. There may be considerable variation within each element, and any one element may be absent altogether. The proportion of each element used in a particular piece will also vary, according to the whim of the designer.

The mesh background is composed of intersecting rows of stitches which are worked diagonally. These are unobtrusive in appearance, as befits their function as a vehicle for the patterned areas.

The open pattern areas generally contain composite stitches such as spiders and rose ground which are often used within a large solid area, or between solid areas and mesh.

The solid pattern areas are worked in horizontal rows, back and forth, and use the most basic of the bobbin lace stitches, each of which has a different density and therefore produces a different texture within the lace.

It is these horizontally worked stitches which are the subject of this chapter. They are common to all styles of bobbin lace, and would form the first lesson for nearly all new lacemakers, whatever they might eventually move on to. If you are only interested in Torchon lace at this stage you may wish to go straight on to Chapter 5, after completing Section 5 of the sampler (see plate 3.1). On the other hand, if you think your interest might be broader than Torchon and you have the time to digress, you could complete Section 6 and work some of the braids which follow in Chapter 4. All would make decorative trimmings for clothing or household linen, as well as giving you valuable practice in the basic stitches and their variations, and introducing you to the possibilities of colour in your lace.

Make the pricking for the first sampler as described in Chapter 2, copying the markings on pattern diagram 3.1. The dots mark the position of the pin holes, and the zigzag line indicates the path of the worker pair. The arrows at

Plate 3.1 *The first sampler*

Diagram 3.1 *Pattern diagram for the first sampler*

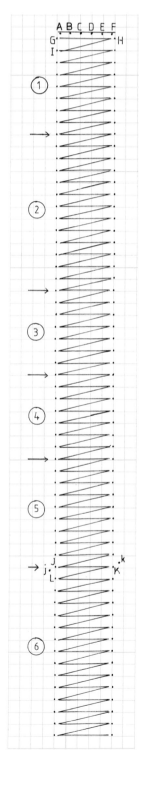

the left hand side mark the end of each section of the sampler. Note that the two vertical rows of dots are 1.5 cm ($^5/_8$") apart, which means that the six top dots (A to F) will have to be spaced by eye.

For the first sampler wind six pairs of bobbins in the main (pale) colour, and one pair in a contrasting colour. Hang the contrast pair around a pin at G, and one of the main colour pairs on a pin in each of the holes A to F. Make sure they all hang with no more than 12 cm (5") of thread between bobbin and pin, and try to maintain this whilst working; if the bobbins hang too far from the work they become unmanageable. Spread the bobbins fanwise on the pillow and leave them for a moment.

You will learn the basic lacemaking movements before you begin the sampler; for that you will need two extra pairs of bobbins, wound with the same coloured thread, and hung on two pins set close together in the pillow, to the left of the other bobbins (see plate 3.2).

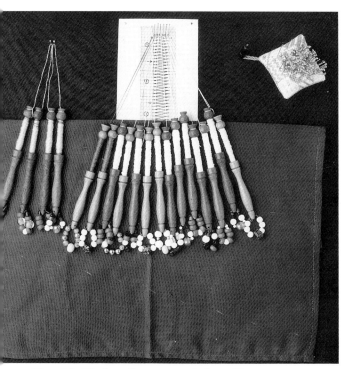

Plate 3.2 *The lace pillow set up ready for working*

The Basic Lacemaking Movements

It always comes as a surprise to new students to learn that the complex and varied stitches of bobbin lace are composed of different combinations of only two basic movements, which are known as the 'cross' and the 'twist'. These basic movements always involve two pairs of threads, so with your extra two pairs on the pillow before you, proceed as follows.

First movement: the cross
Make the first movement by crossing the middle two threads of the four, left over right, with your left hand; that is,

numbering from left to right, pick up no. 2 bobbin with your left hand and place it between no. 3 and no. 4.

Second movement: the twist
Now, with both hands, make the second movement by simultaneously twisting each pair of threads right thread over left thread, that is, re-numbering, again from left to right, move no. 2 bobbin over no. 1 with your left hand, and no. 4 bobbin over no. 3 with your right hand.

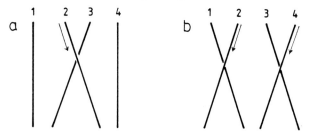

Diagram 3.2 *(a) The cross movement: (b) The twist movement*

Continue, alternating the two movements with these same two pairs of threads until they become quite automatic and you can identify which was the last movement made, should you be interrupted. After a time you will see that you have actually made a four strand plait (diagram 3.3); it is probably rather loose, but tension is not the primary concern at present. Continue plaiting until you feel very confident that you will always CROSS the middle two threads LEFT OVER RIGHT, and TWIST the pairs of threads RIGHT OVER LEFT. You can then remove the extra bobbins and the plait from the pillow.

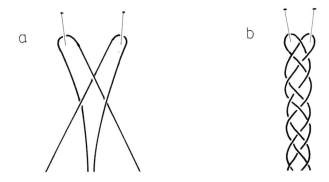

Diagram 3.3 *(a) Cross + twist and (b) the plait made by repeatedly alternating these two basic movements with the same two pairs of threads*

Just as the basic movements always involve two pairs of threads, so also does each stitch. Which stitch you make will depend upon how you combine the movements, and which pairs you use. You have seen that if you repeatedly alternate the cross and twist movements with the same two pairs you will produce a plait (and there are some laces which are made entirely of plaits). In the first sampler you will see what happens when you make different combinations of the two movements, and work the pairs in series.

The First Sampler

Section 1: Cloth stitch (also known as whole or linen stitch)

The first sampler is a braid of basic stitches. The first part of the sampler is worked in cloth stitch which is composed of:

a cross + a twist + a cross;

that is, three movements (but only two different movements) which result in the pair of threads on the left weaving through, and therefore changing places with, the pair on the right (diagram 3.4).

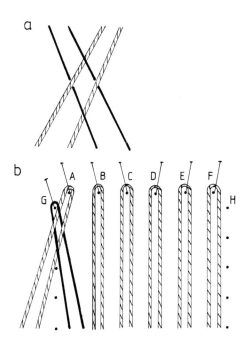

Diagram 3.4 *(a) A cross + a twist + a cross makes a cloth stitch, and (b) the first cloth stitch on the sampler*

The contrast pair of threads, hanging on pin G, will weave back and forth through each of the main colour pairs in turn, and for this reason are known as the 'workers' (or 'weavers' or 'leaders'). The other pairs, which correspond to the warp threads in weaving, are known as the 'passives'. It is hoped that the use of the contrast threads will not only show up your mistakes quickly, but also give you an understanding of the passage of the pairs of threads in each different stitch. If you make a mistake, I suggest that you regard it as part of the learning process and do not attempt to undo it unless it interferes with the pattern of the contrast threads. If you must undo, and the error is several rows back, remove each pin only as you come to it. A dreadful tangle is likely to result if you remove all the necessary pins before you start undoing the stitches.

To start then, take the worker pair on G and first passive pair on A, and make a cloth stitch (cross + twist +

cross). A is now on the left after the stitch, and G is on the right: A is laid aside to the left, and G now makes a cloth stitch with the next passive pair to the right (B) which is, in its turn, laid aside. Continue in this way until the worker pair G has whole-stitched through all six passive pairs, A to F, and now lies to the right of them. Pull the workers up horizontal with your right hand, while holding the passive bobbins taut with the palm of your left hand. Give the worker pair only, one twist (remember, right over left) and pin under it, into the edge hole H, to the right of the last passives worked (diagram 3.5).

Bring the workers down to hang vertically again and whole-stitch them back to the left, being careful *not to reverse the stitch movements*; the leftwards progression is achieved by laying aside the right hand pair, instead of the left hand pair, after each stitch. (It is quite surprisingly difficult to resist reversing the movements.) Having worked through all the passive pairs back to the left edge, again pull the workers up horizontal (with the left hand), twist them once, and pin under them at I to the left of the last passives worked. This extra twist at the pin is the general practice and serves to keep the edge neater and firmer. If you are not careful to twist in the correct direction (right over left) the edge passive thread will come loose when the pins are removed. Return the workers to the vertical and continue weaving back and forth, as for the first two rows, until you have worked 3 or 4 cm (about 1½"), and you feel reasonably confident of the stitch. Finish with the workers on the left hand side, at the pin hole next to the first arrow on the pricking.

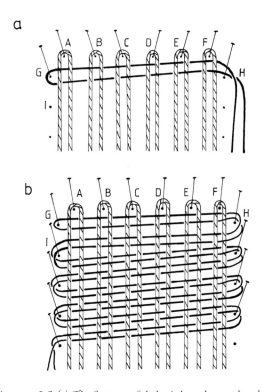

Diagram 3.5 *(a) The first row of cloth stitch on the sampler, showing the position of the pin at the end of the row. (b) The first eight rows of cloth stitch on the sampler*

At this point pause to consider a few extra points which may have occurred to you as you worked.

1. To keep an even tension on your work, gently pull the threads into place at the end of each row. Try not to be timid about doing this; thread of this weight is hard to break.
2. No doubt you will have seen that you need to angle the pins slightly backwards (and outwards as well, at the edges) to keep the stitches well down on the pricking, and to provide enough resistance to tension against. In Torchon lace the pins are pushed into the pillow for about half of their length only.
3. It is most important that you look only at the threads as you work and not at the bobbins; in this way you will learn to recognise the pattern the threads make in each stitch, and will more easily identify a mistake. It is also important that you make all the necessary manipulations of the threads with your hands on the bobbins only. White thread gets very dirty if handled, and even coloured threads acquire an unpleasant used look; but most significantly, your tension will be better if you pull the threads up by the bobbins only. So 'eyes on the thread' and 'hands on the bobbins' should be the rule. This may seem difficult at first, but it should eventually become automatic.

Section 2 : Half stitch (also known as lattice stitch)

Half stitch is made with two movements only:

a cross + a twist

However, instead of repeating these movements with the same two pairs of threads, as you did when you made your beginning plait, you make the progression back and forth through pairs as for cloth stitch, but working each stitch cross + twist, instead of cross + twist + cross (diagram 3.6).

Work the first row of half stitches from left to right, pull up the worker pair, and give it an extra twist (it already had one twist as part of the last stitch). Pin at the edge and pause (diagram 3.7).

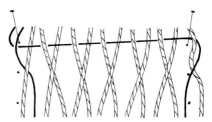

Diagram 3.7 *The first row of half stitch. Note that the contrast thread is the leading thread of the worker pair as it lies ready to work the next row*

You will notice that the threads of the contrast working pair have separated; one was left behind as part of the passive pair laid aside after the first stitch, but the other worked all the way across the row taking a new partner in each stitch. (It is customary still to think in terms of a working pair even though only one thread of that pair is constant.) You will also notice that all of the pairs now lie twisted, and MUST BE LEFT TWISTED, whereas after a row of cloth stitch the threads of the pairs lie parallel. If you continue, working each row as described for the first row, and being careful to include the extra twist at the pin, you should find that the contrast passive thread works diagonally towards the opposite edge of the sampler, while the other contrast thread weaves back and forth horizontally (diagram 3.8).

The diagonal contrast thread shows what happens to each of the passives in turn as it makes its way to the opposite edge of the sampler and back again. (In cloth stitch the passive threads remain vertical.) Once in each row the contrast threads must meet in a stitch, and care must be taken then not to continue with the wrong pair as workers. If all is well, your contrast threads should come together again on the left hand side at the second arrow on the pricking, ready for you to begin Section 3. (They also met on the right hand edge further back.) You are to be congratulated

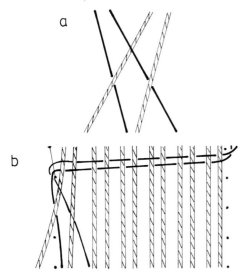

Diagram 3.6 *(a) Half stitch (cross + twist) and (b) the first half stitch on the sampler*

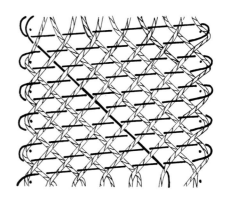

Diagram 3.8 *Several rows of half stitch, with the extra twist on the working pair at the pin; one contrast thread works diagonally and the other works back and forth horizontally*

if you have achieved this without mishap as half stitch is often difficult for beginners to comprehend. If you are having trouble the following may help.

Possibly you found at some stage that you had lost the horizontal thread from the working pair. Generally this happens because the extra twist at the pin has been omitted (or occasionally because there are too many twists at the pin) and does not actually constitute a mistake. It will however, confuse you, so undo back to the pin where the twist was missed and before you proceed again ensure that the contrast thread is the leading thread of the working pair. Diagram 3.9 shows what would have happened if you had consistently omitted the extra twist at the pin from the beginning of the half stitch; the second contrast thread would also have worked diagonally after the first row, and there would also have been a change of working thread at the end of all subsequent rows. This is an acceptable method for working half stitch but it is not as strong as that in which the working thread remains constant throughout.

A very common mistake in half stitch is the 'hole' which appears when one of the passive pairs has been accidentally untwisted before working a stitch. Diagram 3.10 shows how such a mistake would look on your sampler.

If it has not upset the pattern of the contrast threads it may be wise to leave the mistake and work on. If a contrast thread is involved, undo back to the beginning of the row in which the mistake occurred and replace the missing twist. (The pairs should all lie twisted after a row of half stitch.)

If other mistakes develop which you are unable to cor-

rect, and if you have reached the second arrow on the pricking without the contrast threads having come together, simply lift them into the correct position (that is, to the left of the main colour passive pairs) and continue on to Section 3.

Section 3: Cloth-stitch-and-twist, generally abbreviated to cloth-and-twist (also known as whole-stitch-and-twist and double half stitch).

Each cloth-and-twist is worked:

cross + twist + cross + twist

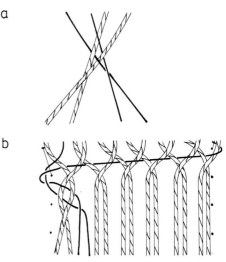

Diagram 3.11 (a) Cloth-and-twist (cross + twist + cross + twist) and (b) the first cloth-and-twist on the sampler

It is a useful stitch and more stable than the first two. Because there is more happening in each stitch (four movements instead of two or three), you will need to pull up after each stitch, as well as at the end of each row, to get a firm neat appearance. Work about 2 cm (³/₄") of this stitch, again finishing with the workers on the left hand side, at the third arrow on the pricking (diagram 3.12).

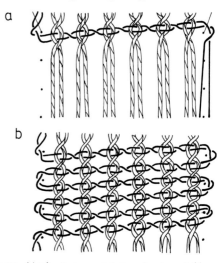

Diagram 3.12 (a) The first row of cloth-and-twist and (b) a number of rows of cloth-and-twist

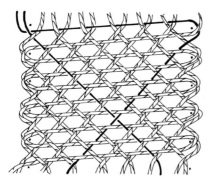

Diagram 3.9 Several rows of half stitch, without the extra twist at the pin; both contrast threads work diagonally after the first row

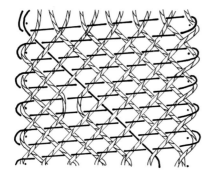

Diagram 3.10 This kind of mistake in half stitch will result if one of the passive pairs becomes untwisted

Section 4: Cloth stitch with cloth-and-twist at the edges[1]

*Make a cloth-and-twist with the workers and first pair of passives, then cloth stitch (cross, twist, cross) through all but the last of the remaining passive pairs; now twist the worker pair only, once, before working it through the last pair of passives in cloth-and-twist; give the workers their extra twist, pin * and repeat from * to * for the next and subsequent rows (diagram 3.13). Pull up the edge stitches well, to make the edge firm. Work about 2 cm (³/₄") of this section, and end with the contrast workers on the left side again, at the fourth arrow on the pricking.

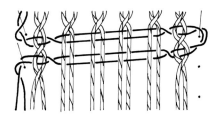

Diagram 3.13 *The first two rows of cloth stitch with cloth-and-twist at the edges*

Section 5: Half stitch with cloth-and-twist at the edges

Work each row of this section as follows:

*Make a cloth-and-twist with the workers and first pair of passives, then half stitch through all but the last pair of the remaining passives; now take the workers through this last pair of passives in cloth-and-twist, give the workers their extra twist, pin * and repeat from * to * for the next and following rows. Note that there is no need to twist the workers before working the edge stitch at the end of a row because they are already twisted as part of the half stitch (diagram 3.14).

Work this section down to pin J, at the fifth arrow on the pricking. By this time the contrast threads should have come together again. If they have not, lift them into position as suggested at the end of Section 3. (If you have had trouble with both half stitch sections you would be wise to work a sampler, just in half stitch, when this one is finished.)

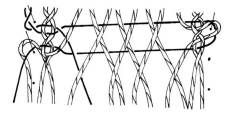

Diagram 3.14 *The first two rows of half stitch with cloth-and-twist at the edges*

Section 6: Adding a footside or straight edge

Cloth-and-twist gives a firm edge to lace but sometimes it is also important to have an edge which is straight, for stitching on to fabric for example. This straight edge is known as a footside.

Wind two more pairs of bobbins, each in a different colour (making three contrasting colours in all) and have these pairs coupled, as were the pairs you started the sampler with (diagram 3.15).

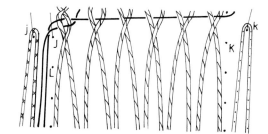

Diagram 3.15 *The new pairs hung on at j and k ready to make a footside on the sampler*

Hang one new pair on j and the other on k: these new pairs are extra working pairs which will alternate with the original worker in the following way, to make a footside on both sides of the sampler. Make a cloth stitch with the new workers on j and the original workers at J. Twist twice the pair now on the left (the original working pair) and lay it aside; then work the right hand (new) pair to the right in cloth stitch through all the passives, and through the new worker pair on k. Twist twice the worker pair now outermost and pin at K *inside* the *two* working pairs (diagram 3.16).

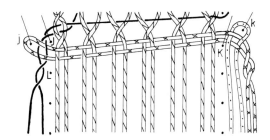

Diagram 3.16 *The first row of Section 6, showing the position of the pin at the end of the first row*

Push aside the outermost pair and work the next pair back to the left in cloth stitch, observing that you have thus alternated the workers at K. The same thing happens at L where you alternate the pair which has come from K with the pair laid aside at J at the beginning of the section. Note that the position of the edge pins is crucial; the edge will not be straight unless the pins are placed *inside* the two edge pairs and *not between* them (diagram 3.17).

At this stage, as you are near the end of the pricking, you may be finding that the bobbins are hard to manage because they are falling off the edge of the pillow. This

---

[1]When cloth-and-twist is used like this the edge is sometimes called a spoke stitch edge.

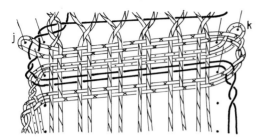

Diagram 3.17 *Several rows of Section 6, showing the alternation of the three working pairs to make the footside or straight edge*

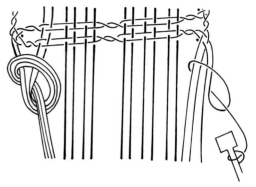

Diagram 3.19 *An overhand knot (left) and a collecting knot (right)*

may be overcome by placing a small cushion under the front edge of the pillow so that it makes a temporary extension to support the bobbins until you have finished the sampler.

Work about 2 cm (³/₄″) of the sampler with the plain footside, then vary the work in the following two ways:

1. Having laid aside the exchanged worker pair with two twists, also twist the other workers twice and cloth stitch them through the passives; again twist the workers twice, then work the 'exchange' cloth stitch; twist both workers twice, pin, and work the inner pair back to the other side. When repeated, this gives an open edge to the sampler and pushes the passives together (diagram 3.18).
2. As well as the open edge, make a pattern in the centre of the sampler by twisting the workers (twice) half way across the row (diagram 3.18).

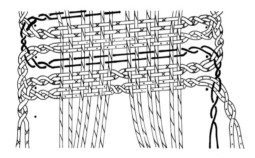

Diagram 3.18 *Opening up the edge of the sampler by twisting both pairs of workers at the ends of the rows. The diagram also shows the beginning of the twist pattern in the centre of the sampler*

Work on until you come to the end of the pattern. Finish the sampler by cutting off the bobbins, leaving about 7 cm of thread, and tying the ends off in groups of four or six with an overhand knot (or collecting knot) before removing the pin. This will be the standard finishing procedure for all the samplers in the book unless otherwise specified (diagram 3.19).

Summary

The first sampler introduced you to the two basic bobbin lace movements, which are made in relation to two pairs of threads:

1. The *cross*, in which the two middle threads (that is, one thread from each pair) are moved left thread over right thread; and
2. The *twist*, in which each pair of threads is moved right thread over left thread.

In the first sampler, you saw how two basic movements were combined to produce the three basic lace stitches.

Cloth stitch: cross + twist + cross
Half stitch: cross + twist
Cloth-and-twist: cross + twist + cross + twist

You also learned how to use cloth-and-twist to give a firm edge to the less stable stitches, and how to give your lace a straight edge (or footside) by the use of alternating working pairs.

You may also have noticed that the cross movement never occurred out of the context of a stitch, but that the twist movement sometimes did. For example:

1. At the end of a row the worker pair, only, had an extra twist round the pin;
2. In Section 4, the workers, only, were twisted before making the edge stitch at the end of a row;
3. In Section 6 the workers were twisted to open up the edge and centre of the sampler.

Other examples of the use of extra twists will be found in the patterns for the braids in the next chapter, which are extensions of the techniques learned in the first sampler.

4 Decorative Braids

Materials:
35/2 or 40/2 linen or no. 12 cotton perle or equivalent
3 mm (8 to the inch) graph paper

The first four braids are worked in cloth stitch, with twists in varying places, and three of them also have a straight edge or footing. Although the examples in the photographs are made in no. 35/2 linen for use as garment trimmings, they could just as easily be made in knitting wool for heavier garments, or in heavy linen or jute thread to make a belt. (Then of course, you would have to enlarge the pattern.) The braids shown in colour on the cover of the book were made in no. 8 cotton perle.

All four braids can be worked on the first sampler pricking (ignoring the arrows and letters jJ, kK and L). If you wish to use up the thread already wound on your bobbins, knot the bobbins together and pin through the knots into the starting holes; this will prevent the knots from moving around and being worked into the lace. Where two or more pairs start at a pin, use only one knot.

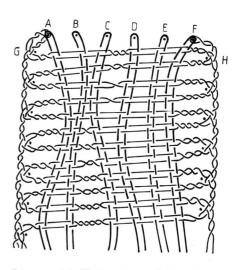

Diagram 4.1 *Working diagram for Braid 1*

Plate 4.1 *Braid 1*

Braid 1

This braid uses six pairs of passives, plus three worker pairs to make the straight edge. Hang (or knot) three pairs around pin A, two pairs around F, and one pair around each of the pins B, C, D and E. The two left hand pairs on A, and the right hand pair on F, are the working pairs. Twist twice the two working pairs on A and work them together in cloth stitch; again twist both pairs twice and leave them to the left of the pin at G, ready to start; it is then the inner pair of these two which will be the working pair for the first row. The working pair on F should also lie twisted twice, ready to be exchanged. If necessary, refer back to Section 6 of the first sampler for the method of alternating these three pairs to make the edge.

The random lozenge pattern of the braid is made by twisting the workers to open up spaces between the passive pairs and to vary the spacing between the passives and the edge. There are two twists throughout on the pair laid aside at the end of each row, and a total of eight or nine twists on the workers in any one row. The actual placement of these twists is for you to decide, but reference to

the diagram and photograph will help. This braid can also be made in two colours; the passives in one colour and the workers in another colour.

Braid 2

This braid has no footside and therefore has only one worker pair in addition to the six passive pairs. Its pattern is made by separating rectangular blocks of cloth stitch with twists.

Hang the six passive pairs on pins A to F, and the worker pair on G. Twist the workers twice to start.

Row 1: taking the workers to the right, cloth stitch twice, twist workers twice, cloth stitch twice, twist workers twice, cloth stitch twice, twist workers three times, pin at edge.

Row 2: working to the left, cloth stitch twice, twist workers twice; cloth stitch once, and twist passive pair twice;

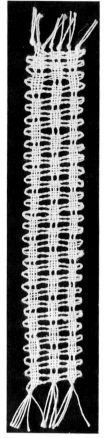

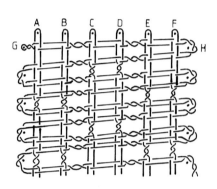

Diagram 4.2 *Working diagram for Braid 2*

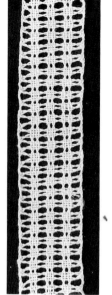

Plate 4.3 *Braid 3*

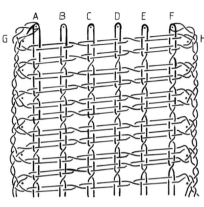

Diagram 4.3 *Working diagram for Braid 3*

Plate 4.2 *Braid 2*

cloth stitch once and twist passives and workers twice; cloth stitch twice, twist workers three times, and pin at the edge, under the workers.

Row 3: work as for Row 1.

Row 4: working left, cloth stitch once and twist passives twice; cloth stitch once and twist passives and workers twice; cloth stitch twice and twist workers twice; cloth stitch once and twist passives twice; cloth stitch once and twist passives twice, and workers three times; pin at the edge, under the workers.

These four rows, repeated, make up the pattern.

Braid 3

This has a footside like the first braid, and therefore also uses three pairs of workers. The pattern is made by separating blocks of four cloth stitches with twists. Prepare to work exactly as for the first braid, excepting that the inner working pair at G has only one twist before starting the first row. If necessary, refer to the first sampler for the method of making the edge.

Row 1: working to the right, cloth stitch twice, twist workers once; cloth stitch twice, twist workers once; cloth stitch twice, twist workers once; now work cloth stitch through the exchange worker (on H for this first row),

and twist the left pair once, and the right pair twice; pin at the edge inside these two pairs. The inner pair of these two is now the worker pair for the next row.

Row 2: working to the left, work as for the first row, but additionally twist each passive pair once after cloth stitching through it. (The passives will be the right hand pair after each stitch.)

These two rows, repeated, make up the pattern.

Braid 4

This braid has a footside on one side only and therefore uses two working pairs which are hung on pin F, together

Plate 4.4 *Braid 4*

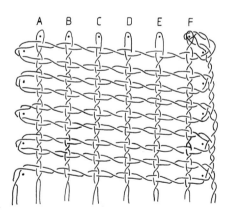

Diagram 4.4 *Working diagram for Braid 4*

with a passive pair. One passive pair also hangs on each of pins A to E inclusive. If you wish, the working pairs may be different colours. Begin working on the right hand side. All the stitches in the braid are cloth-and-twist, with an extra twist on the workers around the pin on the left hand side, and an extra twist on the pair laid aside at the end of the row on the right hand side.

Braid 5

This braid and the following two have scalloped edges and may all be worked from the one pattern. They show how a constant number of pairs can accommodate changes in the width of a lace, either by varying the number of twists on the working pair within the pattern rows, or by using half stitch which is very easily expanded or contracted. (See the cover photograph for colour suggestions.)

For Braid 5 hang one passive pair on each of pins A to D, and a worker pair on E, making five pairs in all.

Row 1: cloth stitch twice, twist the workers once, cloth stitch twice, twist the workers twice, pin at 1.

Row 2: cloth stitch twice, twist the workers twice, cloth stitch twice, twist the workers twice, pin at 2.

Rows 3 to 9 inclusive: cloth stitch twice, twist the workers four times, cloth stitch twice, twist workers twice, pin into the appropriate edge hole.

Row 10: as for row 2, pin at 10.

Repeat the above sequence for the length of the braid.

A wider version of Braid 5 could be threaded with 5 mm ($^3/_8$") ribbon, as shown on the cover, to make a hair band. The pattern is worked as above, with the addition of two extra twists on the workers in the centre of every row. The ribbon is then threaded over three twisted bars and under two.

Braid 6

Hang one passive pair on each of pins A to D, and a worker pair and extra passive pair on E, making six pairs in all. All ten rows of each pattern repeat are worked the same: cloth-and-twist once, half stitch three times, cloth-and-twist once, twist workers once more, pin at the edge. Pull up the edge stitches well to keep the edge firm.

The working of this braid is similar to Section 5 of the first sampler, despite the scalloped edges: no variations are necessary as half stitch is very accommodating on its own.

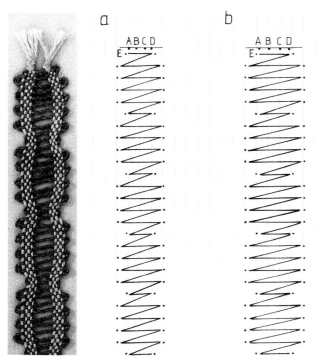

Plate 4.5
Braid 5

Diagram 4.5 (a) Pattern diagram for Braids 5, 6 and 7; (b) Pattern diagram for the wider version of Braid 5

Plate 4.6 Braid 6

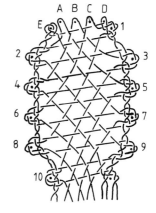

Diagram 4.7 Working diagram for Braid 6

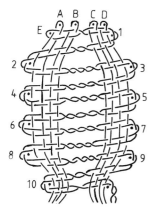

Diagram 4.6 Working diagram for Braid 5

Braid 7

Hang on the five pairs as for Braid 5.

Row 1: cloth-and-twist once, cloth stitch twice, twist the
workers once, cloth-and-twist once, twist the workers
once more, pin at the edge.

Rows 2 to 10 inclusive: cloth-and-twist once, twist the
workers once, cloth stitch twice, twist the workers twice,
cloth-and-twist once, twist the workers once more, pin
at the edge.

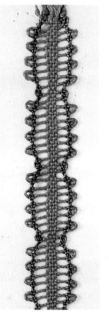

Plate 4.7 *Braid 7*

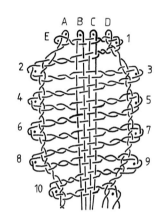

Diagram 4.8 *Working diagram for Braid 7*

5 Torchon Ground Stitches

Materials:
35/2 or 40/2 linen or no. 12 cotton perle or equivalent
3 mm (8 to the inch) graph paper

These ground stitches form the background of most Torchon laces. They are generally worked in diagonal rows rather than horizontally, with a pin in the centre of each stitch instead of the end of each row. A further difference is that the diagonal rows cannot be worked backwards and forwards as were the horizontal rows in the first exercises, but must be worked in one direction only, from the farthest point to the nearest point, on either diagonal. English lacemakers generally work the diagonal rows right down to left but it would be just as correct to work left down to right. For simplicity the exercises will all follow the English method, but I recommend you to be flexible as there is as much European as English influence upon Australian lacemaking.

Before you begin, here are some extra points for you to consider.

1. More about pinning
When making a lace braid which has pins only at the edges, it is sensible to leave all the pins in place until you need to move the work up the pillow, as this ensures that the edges of the braid remain straight. However, when making edgings, and other laces which are pinned in the centre as well as the edges, it is not necessary to leave the pins in more than 6 or 7 cm (about 3") of the lace behind the row upon which you are working. When you have worked such a length, start taking the pins from behind rather than from your pin cushion for succeeding stitches, so that you keep a constant number of pins in the work. This leap-frogging of pins is a common practice in making Torchon lace; it allows you to see the complete lace sooner, free of its forest of pins, and it reduces the number of pins which must be removed when moving up or finishing off.

As the pins are removed you must take care to protect the lace by keeping it covered with one of your working cloths.

2. Coping with a larger number of bobbins
When you worked the first exercises, there were not so many bobbins that you could not keep them all spread out fan-wise before you on the pillow. In the following exercises this will not always be possible, as you will have too many bobbins. If you find this to be the case, push aside the bobbins you are not immediately using, being careful to keep them in their correct order, and stick a hat pin or similar into the pillow in front of them, to keep them out of the way. (Traditionally, ornamental pins called divider pins were used for this purpose.)

The Torchon Ground Sampler

As Torchon meshes are always based on a right-angled diamond grid, patterns can easily be drawn on conventional graph paper, used either diagonally or on the square.

Make the sampler pattern by copying the pattern (diagram 5.1) exactly. Begin with the six dots across the top and the dots along the right and left hand edges. Then add the rest of the dots and the other pattern markings. Make the pricking as described in Chapter 2. The sampler uses fourteen pairs of bobbins in all: ten pairs in the main colour thread, plus two pairs in one contrasting colour, and two pairs in a second contrasting colour. The bobbins need not be coupled for this exercise. Pin the pricking to the pillow and hang on the bobbins as follows, knotted together at each point with a single overhand knot, with the pin through the knot (diagram 5.2).

- At each of A and F hang two pairs in the main colour and one contrasting pair, with the contrasting pair in the middle;
- At each of B and E hang two pairs in the main colour;
- At C and D hang one main colour pair and one contrasting pair (at C the contrast is on the right and at D it is on the left).

Section 1: Simple Torchon ground

Give all the pairs a twist to start with, then work as follows.

Make a half stitch (cross + twist) with the right hand pair from A and the left hand pair from B; pin at 1, between these pairs, and enclose the pin with another half stitch (diagram 5.3).

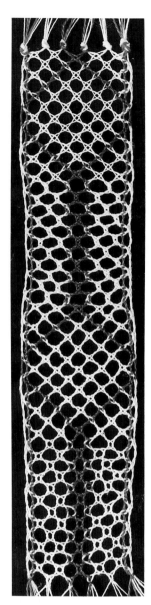

Plate 5.1 *The Torchon Ground Sampler. The wavy edges are due to different rates of contraction of the stitches once the pins are removed*

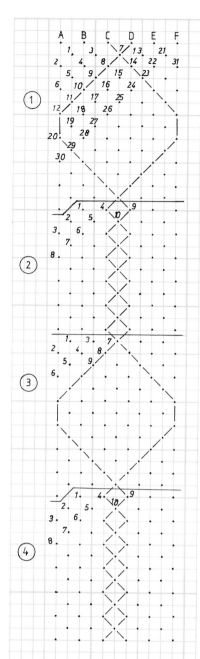

Diagram 5.1 *Pattern diagram for the Torchon Ground Sampler*

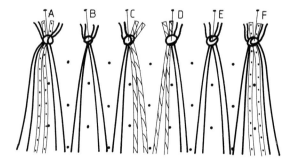

Diagram 5.2 *The bobbins hung ready to start the Torchon sampler*

The Torchon edge

(The Torchon edge is also called the Torchon footside. It serves the same purpose as the footside in section 6 of the first sampler and looks similar. The difference is that the rows of stitches leading to the edge pin in the Torchon sampler are worked diagonally instead of horizontally.)

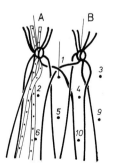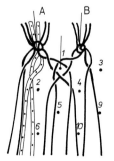

Diagram 5.3 *Simple Torchon ground; half stitch, pin, half stitch*

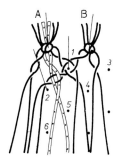
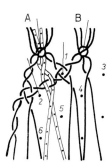
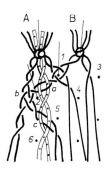

Diagram 5.4 *The three stitches of the Torchon edge*

Pin 2 is an edge pin. All edge pins will be worked identically on both sides of the work. There are three stitches around an edge pin, worked as follows (diagram 5.4).

Work only with the three pairs nearest the edge. Make sure that the outside pair has two twists (to make the edge firmer), and the others one twist each, and that the contrast pair is the centre pair of the three.

Then: with the two inner pairs work cloth-and-twist and pin at 2 between these pairs. Do not enclose the pin at this stage.

Now: work cloth-and-twist with the two outer pairs, laying aside the pair now outermost with an extra twist.

And finally: work cloth-and-twist with the two inner pairs to enclose the pin.

If this procedure is followed exactly you should find that the edge pin is enclosed by three stitches (a, b and c on the diagram) which form a small triangle, and that the contrasting pair lies inside the pin as the middle pair of the three edge pairs, both before and after working the three edge stitches. The whole point of the Torchon edge is to

negotiate the passage of this contrasting pair as passives down the length of the work, to give firmness to the edge which would otherwise stretch, as all the other pairs in the sampler work diagonally. All the edge pins of the Torchon sampler are worked in this manner, regardless of any changes which may be made to the ground stitches.

To continue the ground stitches (diagram 5.5):

For pin 3, take the pair remaining at B and the left pair from C and work half stitch, pin, half stitch;

At 4, take the right hand pair from 1 and the left pair from pin 3 and work half stitch, pin, half stitch;

At 5, take the right hand pair from 2 (not the contrast pair) and the left hand pair from 4 and work half stitch, pin, half stitch;

Pin 6 is a Torchon edge pin, again made with the three outermost pairs (refer back to the notes on the Torchon edge).

Continue working thus, in diagonal rows, following the numbered order. By the time you come to the end of the numbers, the pattern of working should have become clear to you, and you will be able to continue working diagonally, top right down to bottom left, taking one pair from the nearest stitch to the right above, and the other from the nearest stitch to the left above, for each new ground stitch to be worked. Note that after the Torchon edge pin has been worked at the beginning of a row on the right hand edge, it will be the innermost pair of the three which then works in to the ground. To finish each section of the sampler at the horizontal line marked on the pattern, work each diagonal down to, and including, the pin hole immediately above the line. At the end of the first section you should find that the central contrast pairs have made the same diamond-shaped pattern as that in the first section of the photographed sampler. The path followed by each of these contrast pairs reflects what happens to all of the pairs in turn.

If you find that you have made a mistake which affects the colour pattern and you are unable to correct it, try to continue, making the stitches correctly, with the contrasting threads in their new 'accidental' position. The use of coloured threads is meant only to help, not to torment, and as long as you are reasonably confident that you

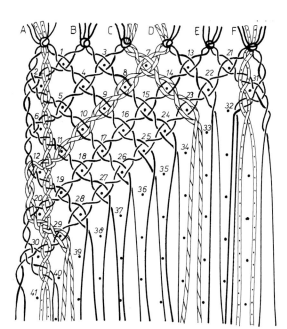

Diagram 5.5 *The first section of the Torchon sampler, up to and including the first edge pin on the right hand side (pin 31).*

understand what you are doing, the mistake will not particularly matter; preserving the colour pattern is not, after all, the primary object of the exercise.

Section 2: Torchon double ground
(The numbers on the pattern begin again to indicate the order of working for the start of each new section.)

Each double ground stitch is worked cloth-and-twist, pin, cloth-and-twist, that is, exactly double the first ground stitch, hence its name (diagram 5.6). Remember, the edge pins are worked as described in the first section, whatever the ground stitch.

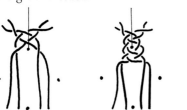

Diagram 5.6 *Torchon double ground; cloth-and-twist, pin, cloth-and-twist*

Continue the diagonal rows down to the next horizontal line. The middle contrast pairs should have diverged by only one pin hole from the centre line before converging again, making a coloured band in the centre of the sampler. (See the second section of the sampler in plate 5.1.)

Section 3: Torchon with two twists
This stitch is worked as for simple Torchon ground but with an extra twist between the pins; that is, half stitch, pin, half stitch, twist, at each pin hole (diagram 5.7). The colour pattern will be the same as in Section 1. Note that after an edge pin is worked on the right hand side of this section, the innermost pair should have an extra twist, two in all, before it works down the diagonal row of ground stitches, to be consistent with the rest of the ground. (It

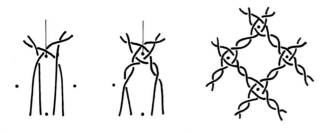

Diagram 5.7 *Torchon with two twists; half stitch, pin, half stitch, twist*

will always be the case that pairs entering and leaving the ground receive the same number of twists as the prevailing ground stitch.)

Section 4: Twisted half stitch ground
This stitch has an extra twist around the pin; that is, half stitch, twist, pin, half stitch (diagram 5.8). The colour pattern will be the same as for Section 2. Work this section to the end of the pattern, and finish off as for the first sampler.

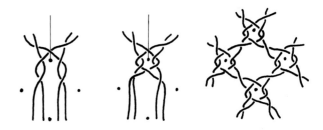

Diagram 5.8 *Twisted half stitch ground; half stitch, twist, pin, half stitch*

'Workers', 'Passives' and 'Ground'

It may be appropriate at this stage to clarify the specific use of the terms 'workers', 'passives' and 'ground', which often confuse new lacemakers.

The term 'workers' or 'working pair' describes a pair of threads whose use predominates over the use of all other pairs within the lace (or section of lace) because it is involved in every stitch. A worker pair usually travels horizontally, back and forth through each of the other pairs in turn, whose role is passive, hence their name. Each passive pair is worked only once in every row. It follows from this that the terms 'worker' and 'passive' are only relevant within blocks of cloth stitch, half stitch, or cloth-and-twist (and their combinations). These stitches might form the whole of a piece of lace, as in the braids of Chapter 4, or they may form only part of it, as in the headside of the edgings in the next chapter.

Although you began this chapter with a complete sampler of ground stitches, the term 'ground' is generally applied only to the net background of laces such as the edgings and insertions in the following chapters. In most Torchon grounds all the pairs of threads involved are equally active. There are therefore no workers as such, and the only passives are edge pairs which, although necessary to stop the lace from stretching, are not part of the structure of the ground.

6 Three Simple Edgings

Materials:
35/2 or 40/2 linen or no. 12 cotton perle or equivalent
3 mm (8 to the inch) graph paper

All three edgings may be worked from the one pattern (diagram 6.1) which is designed to show how the horizontally worked stitches of the scalloped braids may be combined with the diagonally worked ground stitches. The pattern diagram shows the stages in construction as well as the finished pattern. Make the pattern and pricking as before, and pin it to the pillow.

Note that the scalloped edge has six pins to each repeat, where the braids had five, to enable the correct sequence of link stitches with the ground, as well as the right density of horizontal rows for the given diagonal mesh. The line down the centre of the pattern indicates the division between the net ground and the patterned edge band (the headside). The zigzag line within the headside has the same meaning as in previous patterns. To avoid confusion, the finished pattern, d, omits the pin holes above the starting line, but adds two extra support pins (B and C) for the headside passives, to make starting easier.

The number of pairs of bobbins necessary is calculated by allowing two pairs for each pin hole, or pin hole position, on the underlying grid, across the widest part of the pattern (five in this instance) and adding one extra pair as passives for the Torchon edge. This makes eleven pairs in all, which may be knotted or coupled. The bobbins are hung on the pricking in the same way for all three edgings; one pair at A, and two pairs at each of B, C, D, E and F.

The First Edging

The pairs at D, E and F should each have two twists to start with. The ground stitches to the right of the centre line are Torchon with two twists and the footside edge is the standard Torchon edge (refer to the Torchon sampler). The headside is worked in cloth stitch, the workers (from A) being twisted half way through the passives in either direction, as in the working diagram, to make the pattern. See plate 6.1 and diagram 6.2. Refer also to Braid 5 in Chapter 4.

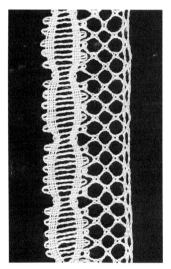

Plate 6.1 *The First Edging*

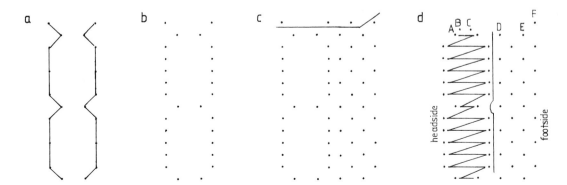

Diagram 6.1 *Stages in making the pattern for the edgings. Extend as required*

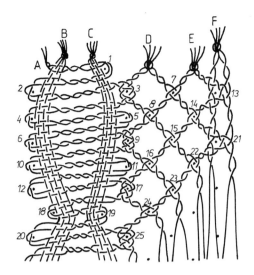

Diagram 6.2 *Working diagram for the First Edging*

Take the workers from A across to pin 1, back to pin 2, and across to pin 3 where the headside joins the ground (three rows). At this point twist the headside workers once and work them through the left hand ground pair at D, in cloth-and-twist. Pin between these pairs at 3, and enclose the pin with another cloth-and-twist. The headside workers have now turned around the pin ready to work back to the outer headside edge; the other pair is left aside to work into the ground and therefore needs an extra twist. You can now work the next four rows of the headside, negotiating pins 4, 5 and 6, and across to, but not including, pin 9, which cannot be worked until the ground stitches 7 and 8 have been made. Pin 9 is then negotiated in the same way as pin 3, and you should follow this by working the next four headside rows around pins 10, 11, 12 and across to pin 17 which can't be worked until the ground stitches 13 to 16 have been made. A rhythmical and efficient pattern of working is thus established, in which one diagonal row of ground stitches is followed by four rows of the headside, throughout the length of the lace. Care must be taken on the inner edge of the headside whenever the workers turn around the pin without involving a pair from the ground (pins 1, 5, 11 and 19 in the diagram); at these points you should check that you have worked through the four passive pairs only, before pinning.

The suggested order of working follows the standard lacemaking practice of working alternate sections of ground and headside, working on the one until involvement of the other is necessary. The bobbins of the section not being worked can be carefully pushed aside, not only to make more working space, but also to ensure that they are not accidentally worked before they should be.

The Second Edging

The pairs on D, E and F each have one starting twist. The order of working is the same as for the first edging, but the stitches are different. The ground stitches are twisted half stitch (see the Torchon sampler) and the headside is worked in half stitch, with cloth-and-twist at the five most prominent headside edge pins of each repeat (slightly different from Braid 6). These are pins 2, 4, 6, 10, 12 and 20 in the working diagram, and are worked as for the edge in Section 5 of the first sampler. Remember that there should be an extra twist on the headside working pair each time it passes around a pin, so that the horizontal working thread remains constant. When this edging is worked in finer

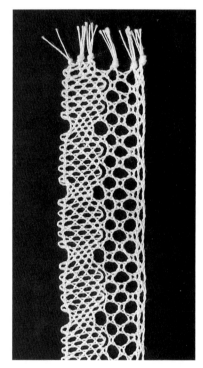

Plate 6.2 *The Second Edging*

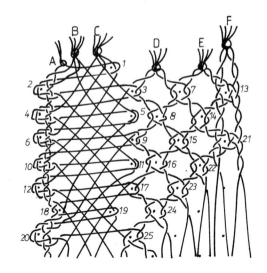

Diagram 6.3 *Working diagram for the Second Edging*

thread, or in thread which is smoother than cotton perle, it may be advisable to add an extra headside passive pair at C.

The Third Edging

The headside of this edging is closely related to Braid 7 in Chapter 4. The pairs on D, E and F should each have one starting twist. The ground stitch is Torchon double ground (again, refer to the Torchon sampler) and the headside is in cloth stitch with whole-stitch and-twist at the edges. Careful study of diagram 6.4 and plate 6.3 should give you all the information you need. The working order is the same as for the first two edgings.

A pleasing variation can be made to this edging by using a contrasting colour for the left hand passive pair on B, and for the right hand passive pair on C.

If the method of calculating the number of pairs puzzled you, diagram 6.5 illustrates an alternative way of arriving at the same edging pattern which may explain the matter more clearly. It starts with a basic mesh strip five pins wide; after marking in the scalloped headside shape, the pin holes within this are removed. The calculation re- lies on the essential fact of Torchon lace that however many pin holes are added or removed from the basic mesh strip to make the design the same number of pairs will gener- ally be needed. Occasionally extra pairs may be added, especially to the headside, but you will never need less than you would for a strip of plain mesh of the same size.

If you are still puzzled, do not worry. All is explained more fully in Chapter 19, Beginnings and Endings, and will make a lot more sense when you have drawn more patterns and made more lace.

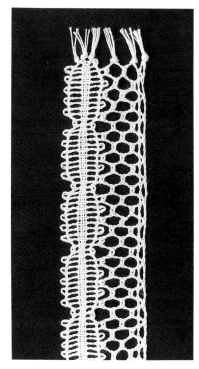

Plate 6.3 *The Third Edging*

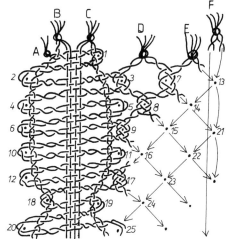

Diagram 6.4 *Working diagram for the Third Edging*

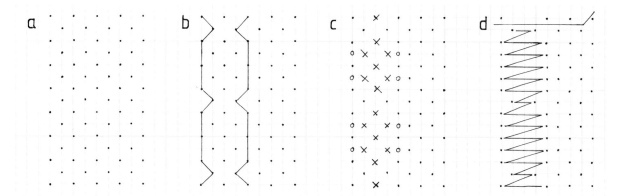

Diagram 6.5 *An alternative method of constructing the edgings pattern. In (c) the crosses indicate pin holes left out of the grid and circles indicate extra pin holes added*

7 Graph Paper, Thread and Pattern Making

Choice of Thread

For reductions of the exercises in this book, and for fine laces generally, linen thread is undoubtedly the most suitable material to use. Linen wears well and keeps its shape and crispness through repeated launderings. However, many people do not like using the finer linen threads because they are uneven and break easily if the lacemaker does not have a sufficiently delicate touch. Cotton thread is then the only readily available alternative. Suitable varieties are the finer crochet or tatting cottons (size 70 or finer) and the different machine embroidery threads. There are also ultra fine lacemaking cottons available from the specialist lacemakers' suppliers. This chapter suggests only a few of the possibilities.

Should you wish to enlarge the given patterns there are so many threads available that it is only practical here to mention a few of the possibilities. As well as the heavier threads made specifically for lacemaking, many of the knitting cottons work well, as do weaving linens and the heavier perle cottons.

Comparing Thread Sizes

The numbering of sizes in commercial yarn can be very confusing to anyone who has not previously been involved in a textile craft. In general the lower the number the thicker the thread because the number refers to the number of hanks of a certain length in 1 pound (454 grams) of a single ply of the yarn. Unfortunately it is not possible at present to equate threads of different fibre composition as the length measures are different. For example, the measure for linen is the number of 300 yard (270 metre) hanks per pound (454 grams) of single ply yarn and for cotton it is the number of 840 yard (757 metre) hanks to the pound. For wool and silk it is different again.

Because of the confusion this causes, in industry as well as to the consumer, some years ago there was an international industry agreement to standardise yarn counts (and yarn labelling) for all fibres, including synthetics. Unfortunately this only seems to work in industry. The old system seems to continue for the domestic market. To lacemakers this means that we cannot substitute say, no. 80 crochet cotton for no. 80 linen, or no. 8 cotton perle for no. 8 knitting cotton, unless we are prepared to alter the scale of our patterns.

The Twist of the Thread

As well as the size of the thread you choose you should also consider its twist. Specialist bobbin lacemaking thread is almost always composed of two or three single threads spun with a Z twist and twisted together with an S twist to make the finished yarn. Lacemaking thread needs a tighter finishing twist than S twisted embroidery or weaving yarn because some of the twist is lost during the lacemaking process. It is quite alright to use the softer spun yarn as long as you stop every so often and give each bobbin a few turns to the right to restore its twist.

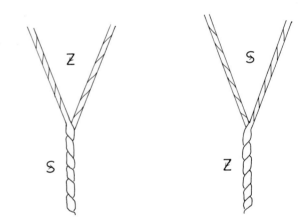

Diagram 7.1 *S twisted thread (left) and Z twisted thread (right)*

I know that it is not always possible to find S twisted thread, especially in the finer sizes. Z twisted thread is perfectly acceptable, especially if it has a relatively soft twist. Machine embroidery thread (not ordinary sewing thread) is a good example of softly spun Z twist thread. However, because the twist on this thread is *increased* during the lacemaking process you would be well advised to minimise the number of twists you use in your stitches. For example, if it is possible to work ground stitches with one twist or two, choose one. The accumulated result of too many twists in lace made with Z twisted thread causes the lace to lose its shape once the pins are removed, or when it is washed.

The table on pages 40–41 is a guide to the kinds of threads suitable for different sizes of pattern grid. It is by no means exhaustive in its suggestions, but you will find it useful as a reference while you are learning the craft. Eventually your own experience will be your best guide.

Graph Paper and Pattern Making

All Torchon laces are based on a diamond mesh grid, which can be plotted on standard graph paper, and the size of the mesh depends upon the weight of the thread to be used. You will absorb quite a lot about the construction of a lace pattern on a basic mesh grid, just by copying the various patterns and working the laces. However, if eventually you want the freedom of designing your own patterns, or reducing those given, a more formal understanding of the use of graph paper and its relationship to thread size is necessary.

So far, to produce patterns suitable for the recommended thread, all exercises have been drafted on 8 to the inch (3 mm) graph paper. The basic grid was plotted over 2 squares of the paper, giving a measurement of 1/4" or 6 mm from pin hole to pin hole, vertically or horizontally, for any one (diamond) unit of the grid. It is more usual to express this as the distance between the footside pin holes, as this is the most convenient part of the pattern to measure when deciding what thread to use. You could produce the same size of grid using 2 mm graph over 3 squares of the paper, as shown in diagram 7.2. This is not nearly as easily or accurately done because you have to mark the centre of each square in alternate rows, but 2 mm graph is often more easily found than 8 to the inch. You could also produce an acceptable (slightly smaller) grid for the given thread by using 10 to the inch graph diagonally.

Before metrication a wide variety of sizes of graph paper was available and most lacemakers drafted their patterns using the graph paper on the square. Since metrication the only graphs readily available are 1 mm, 5 mm, and 2 mm. The computer industry still uses 10 to the inch graph, and weavers use 8 to the inch, so these are usually obtainable as a special order from stationers and art suppliers, but generally speaking imperial graph paper is not easy to find in Australia. It is therefore sensible to learn to use the few available graph papers in different ways to produce the variety of meshes necessary for different thicknesses of thread. This means that you will need to be able to use the graphs both on the square, and diagonally. (When using a graph diagonally you will find it helpful to rule a line to define the edge of the pattern.) To draw the patterns in this book to the given scale you will mostly use the graph paper on the square. If you wish to vary the scale of the patterns you may need to use a particular graph paper diagonally. The following table shows how to draft the basic mesh on different graphs, and indicates what threads would be suitable for each. The list of threads is by no means exhaustive but if you collect at least a small sample of each you will then have a basis for comparison with any other thread you may come across.

Whatever the orientation of the graph paper bear in mind that all Torchon lace has an underlying diamond grid (diagram 7.3). For this reason using the graph paper diagonally is, in my opinion, more logical and should be simpler than using it on the square, but I have observed during many years of teaching that new lacemakers find it difficult to use the graph diagonally.

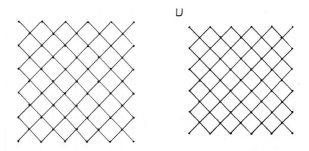

Diagram 7.3 *Whatever the orientation of the graph paper the underlying torchon grid is diamond-shaped*

In the following chapters the construction of each pattern will be described fully as it is presented. I hope that by the end of the book you will understand enough to be able to make a pattern for a simple lace from a photograph. In the meantime, if you see a piece of lace you think you could copy, or if you would like to experiment with a simple design of your own, go ahead.

On the other hand, if the whole subject of pattern construction is still a mystery to you, do not worry. Many people find it difficult to grasp at first, but you may be assured that understanding will come with practice.

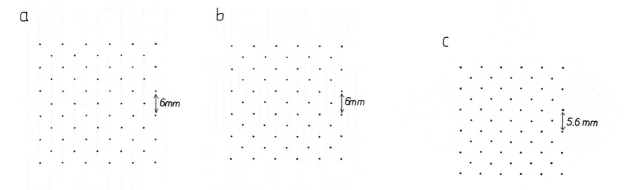

Diagram 7.2 *(a) A 6 mm pattern grid produced by using 3 mm (8 to the inch) graph over 2 squares.*
(b) A grid of the same size produced by using 2 mm graph over 3 squares. (c) A slightly smaller grid (which could still be used with the same size of thread) produced by using 10 to the inch graph diagonally over 2 squares

Table of Grids for Use with Different Threads

Graph	Usage	Mesh/grid size	Threads
5 mm	square	10 mm	No. 5 cotton perle Most fine baby knitting yarns
2 mm	square	8 mm	No. 8 cotton perle 30/2 or 35/2 linen 40/3 or 50/3 linen No. 18 coton à broder
or 5 mm	diagonal	7 mm	
8 to the inch (1/8" or 3 mm)	square	6 mm	No. 12 cotton perle 60/3 linen 40/2 linen 35/2 linen
or 2 mm	square (2 spaces)	5.6 mm	

Graph	Usage	Mesh/grid size	Threads
or 2 mm	square (3 spaces)	6 mm	
10 to the inch (1/10" or 2.5 mm)	square	5 mm	50/2 or 60/2 linen 70/2 Irish linen No. 12 Madeira Tanne
8 to the inch (1/8"or 3 mm)	diagonal	4.2 mm	80/2 linen DMC fil à dentelles No. 100 Mercer Crochet No. 30 Retors d'Alsace No. 30 Brillante d'Alsace No. 100/3 Güttermann silk sewing thread
or 2 mm	square	4 mm	
or 10 to the inch (2/10" or 2.5 mm)	diagonal	3.5 mm	
2 mm	diagonal	2.8 mm	140/2 linen No. 50 Retors d'Alsace No. 80 Brok cotton No. 80 Honiton thread

8 Spiders

Bookmark with Spiders

Materials:
35/2 or 40/2 linen or no. 12 cotton perle, or equivalent
3 mm (8 to the inch) graph paper

This lesson makes use of the techniques learned in the basic samplers and introduces the decorative 'spider' motif often seen in Torchon lace. The spiders are separated by diagonal rows of ground stitches, and contrasting threads are used to give them emphasis, and to help you understand them. The bookmark has a wide border in cloth-and-twist (plate 8.1).

CONSTRUCTION OF THE BOOKMARK PATTERN
The main aim of this exercise is to introduce spider motifs through the smallest possible spider, and the strategic use of coloured threads. To show you a different edge finish, and to give you the satisfaction of working a complete article, I have added a border to the basic design to make it into a pattern for a bookmark (diagram 8.1).

The smallest possible spider involves four pairs of threads, and is worked within a diamond bounded by twelve pin holes of the standard Torchon grid (part a of the diagram); the four pin holes normally inside the diamond are replaced by a single centre pin hole. Take this as the basic pattern unit and add to it groups of three spider diamonds, arranged chevron fashion (b); this will give a repeating sequence in which the contrasting pairs pass from a centre spider out to the side spiders and inwards again to the next centre spider, for the length of the bookmark.

Next mark in the pin holes vertically on a line connecting the side points of the design to complete the inner edge of the border; it then only needs a second line of pin holes parallel with this to make the outer edge of the border (c). The most pleasing width for the border seems to be 1 cm (³/₈"). The finished pattern is then ten pin holes wide and will use exactly twenty pairs of bobbins since it will not be worked with a Torchon edge.

Part d of the diagram shows the final pattern of pin

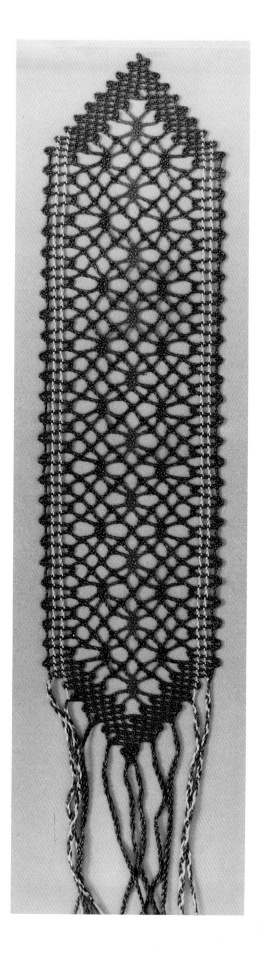

Plate 8.1 *The Spiders Bookmark*

Diagram 8.1 *Stages in the construction of the pattern diagram for the Spiders Bookmark. Part e is the completed pattern*

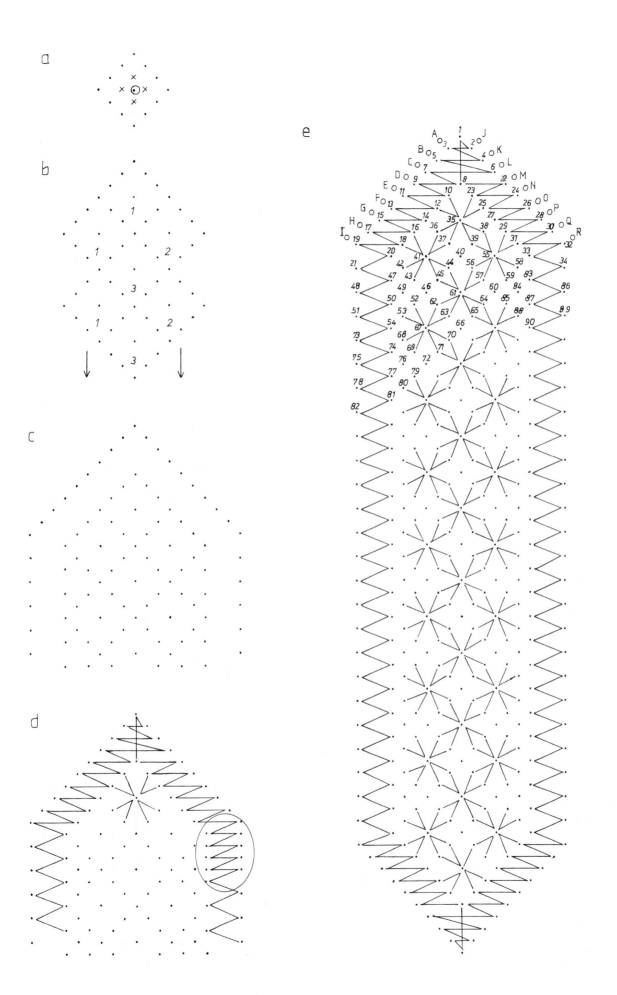

holes. Strictly speaking, to maintain the same density of rows as in the top border of the bookmark, extra pin holes should also have been added between those of the side borders (inset, part d). However, having decided to use cloth-and-twist for the border, I felt that extra rows would have crowded the stitches too much; as it is some may find it difficult to work the top stitches neatly. (Perhaps you would like to try a second bookmark, with a cloth stitch border and with the extra pin holes, just to see the effect.)

Part e of the diagram shows the completed pattern. The markings within the diamonds of the centre section of the pattern are the standard method of indicating spiders, and the zigzag lines in the border represent the passage of the two border working pairs. Again the numbers indicate the order of working the pins.

As you can see, the construction and design of the bookmark pattern was approached in a similar way to that of the Chapter 6 edgings in that the main features of the design were marked out first and allowed to determine subsequent details. This is probably the most common approach, and the quickest. The other method, described at the end of Chapter 6, in which the whole grid is marked out first and the design arrived at by a process of elimination or addition of pin holes in key places, is probably more logical but takes much longer.

Make the pricking in the usual way. Pin the pricking to the pillow and place pins in the circles A to I, and J to R. These are temporary pins which will support bobbins whilst they are being worked into the lace. Also put in pin 1.

Twenty pairs of bobbins will be used, including eight contrasting pairs. Each pair must be coupled, and with the exception of the two border working pairs, each bobbin needs only 1 metre of thread (about 1 yd). The border workers need 2 metres (2 yds) of the main colour thread on each bobbin, and should be hung one inside the other around top pin 1 (diagram 8.2); the new pairs thus formed each need one twist ready to start. Now hang a main colour pair on each of the temporary pins C, D, E, F, I and L, M, N, O, R and on each of the remaining eight temporary pins hang a contrasting pair.

Every stitch in the border is a cloth-and-twist, and all the ground stitches around the spiders are Torchon with two twists (Section 3, Torchon Sampler, page 33). As you work, make careful reference to the photograph, and to the working diagrams. Do not forget the extra twist on the

workers at the pin.

To begin, enclose pin 1 with a cloth-and-twist (following diagram 8.3). The pair now on the left is temporarily passive, and the right hand pair is taken as the working pair, to the right through the new pair on J, in cloth-and-twist; pin at 2 between the pairs, and make another cloth-and-twist to enclose the pin. Now remove the temporary pin at J and pull the new pair down into place at pin 2. Work left in cloth-and-twist through the other pair from 1, and bring in the new pair on A at pin 3, as for pin 2. Work back and forth in cloth-and-twist, bringing in the new pairs on K, B, L and C at pins 4, 5, 6 and 7. After pin 7, work to the right through four pairs only; pin at 8, between the workers and the fourth passive pair, and enclose the pin with another cloth-and-twist. The pair on the left after this stitch continues as the worker pair down the left hand border, and the right hand pair, originally from pin 1 and passive until now, becomes the worker pair for the right hand border.

Continue the border to pin 21 on the left side and pin 34 on the right side, bringing in the new pairs from the temporary pins as already described, and leaving a pair out at each of the pins 10, 12, 14, 16, 18, 20 and 23, 25, 27, 29, 31, 33 on the inside of the border. The pairs left out should have two twists each, ready to work the centre section of the bookmark.

After pins 21 and 34 the border workers should be taken back through the passives and left ready to work pins 47 and 83 respectively, when the appropriate ground pairs become available.

You are now ready to work the first spider around pin 35. The working diagram for the top of the bookmark shows this spider completed, so that you can see how the pairs from pins 10 and 12 on the left, and 23 and 25 on the right, work through each other, pass around the central pin, then work back through each other again, emerging from the spider on the same side as they started, but below the central pin. The four pairs from the spider are then taken into the rows of ground stitches which separate it from the spiders below.

In more detail the procedure is as follows. Working only with the pairs from 10 and 12, 23 and 25, cloth stitch the pair from 23 through the pair from 10 and through the pair from 12, making stitches 1 and 2 as in diagram 8.4. Then do the same with the pair from 25, making 3 and 4. Pin at 35 in the centre of the four pairs; tension the threads carefully, and the work should appear as in part d of diagram 8.4.

Now, to take the pairs back again, work the pair immediately to the left of the pin in cloth stitch through the two pairs to the right of the pin, making 5 and 6. Finally, work the other left hand pair through the two right hand pairs, making 7 and 8. Give all four pairs two twists to match the twists they started with, and the spider is now complete (part g of diagram 8.4).

Then, with the pair from 14 and the outer left pair from the spider (originally from 12), make the ground stitch at

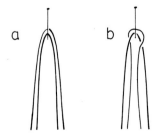

Diagram 8.2 *The pairs on pin 1, ready to start*

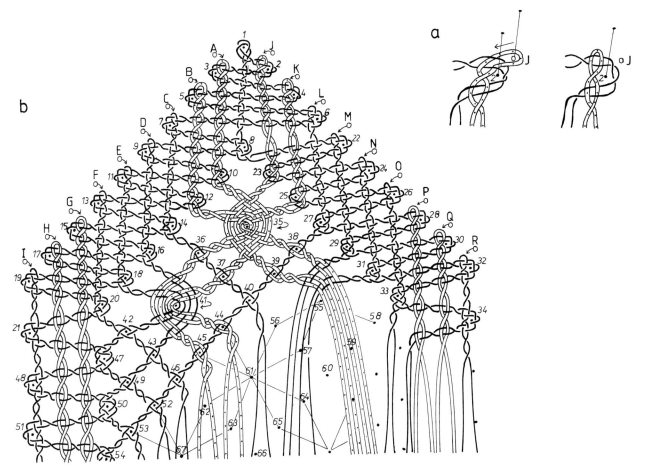

Diagram 8.3 *(a) The method of bringing in a new pair from a temporary pin; (b) Working diagram for the top of the bookmark*

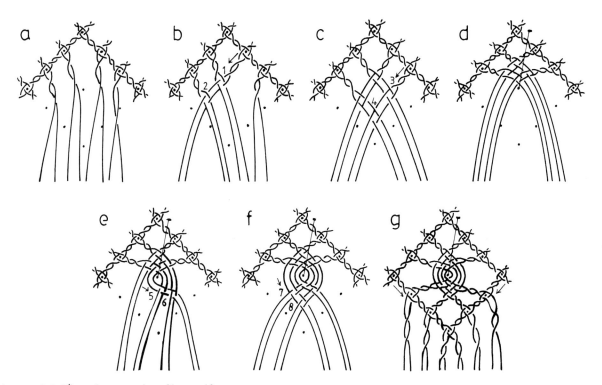

Diagram 8.4 *The various stages in making a spider*

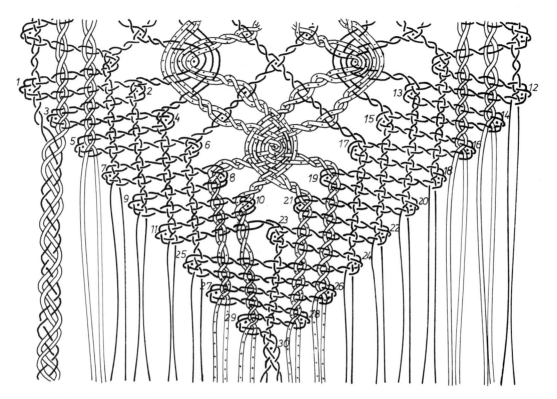

Diagram 8.5 *Working diagram for the bottom of the bookmark*

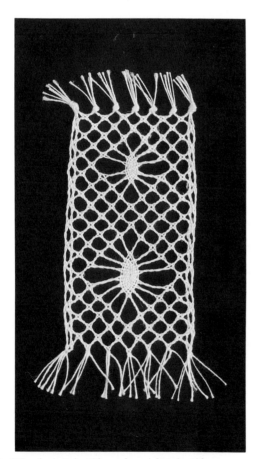

Plate 8.2 *A six-pair spider and an eight-pair spider*

Diagram 8.6 *Pattern diagram for a lace sampler containing a six-pair spider and an eight-pair spider. Note the alternative pattern marking for spiders*

36 (half stitch, pin, half stitch, twist). Work 37 with the inner left pair from the spider (originally from 10) and the right hand pair from 36. Next, work pin 38 with the outer right hand pair from the spider (originally from 25) and the pair from 27; then work 39 with the last remaining pair from the spider (from 23 originally) and the left hand pair from 38. Finally, work pin 40 with the left pair from 39, and the right pair from 37. The other spiders in the bookmark are all worked in a similar way.

As well as the rows of ground stitches separating the spiders, there are also single ground stitches at 49 and 69, and their corresponding pins in the rest of the bookmark. Note also that the pairs brought in at G, H, I and P, Q, R work down the edges of the bookmark as passives in the border.

The bottom of the bookmark is worked the reverse of the top, pairs being taken out progressively. Follow carefully the numbers and stitches in diagram 8.5. After pin 11 take the left hand border workers to the right through four pairs, and leave them ready to work pin 23, when the bottom right hand border has also been worked to this point, through pins 12 to 22. The border working pairs then work together around pin 23, after which the left hand border workers become passive and the right hand workers continue as the only working pair to the end of the bookmark.

Before cutting off the bobbins, plait the threads together in fours (remember, a plait is made by half-stitching continuously with the same two pairs) to the length desired. Cut off and tie each plait with a collecting knot.

Larger Spiders

Spiders made with more than four pairs of threads are also frequently found in Torchon lace, and the principle of working them is the same as for the four-pair spider, excepting that the legs of a larger spider will need more twists. A good general rule is to twist as many times as there are legs (pairs) touching each side of the enclosing diamond. Diagram 8.6 is a pattern for a short sampler of lace containing a six-pair spider and an eight-pair spider. The markings on the pattern diagram are an alternative and perhaps more expressive way of indicating spiders. See if you can work this sample, without further information, in one colour and with a Torchon edge. To work the spiders apply the principles inherent in the four-pair spider; to find out how many pairs of bobbins you will need, refer back to the Torchon sampler where you will observe that each top pin of the pattern needed two pairs, plus an extra pair for each of the top edge pins. If you wish you may knot the pairs together to start. Good luck!

The most important observation to make about any spider is that the pairs enter from either side of the top of the diamond, and leave from either side of the bottom; each side of the enclosing diamond must therefore have enough pin holes to accommodate half of the total number of pairs involved in the spider, excluding the pin holes at the points of the diamond. There is theoretically no limit to the size of the spider you could make, but if you get too carried away you might have some interesting structural problems!

9 Cloth and Half Stitch Diamonds

Materials:
50/2 or 60/2 linen, or no. 12 Madeira Tanne or equivalent
2.5 mm (10 to the inch) graph paper

Many motifs in Torchon lace are diamond shaped, and for diamonds of a given size there are often several different stitch possibilities. To demonstrate this the patterns for the two insertions in this chapter are based upon the same arrangement of diamond shapes as for the centre of the bookmark in the previous chapter, with a Torchon edge instead of the whole-stitch-and-twist border, and diamonds of cloth stitch or half stitch in place of some of the central spiders. Later in the book you will find other stitches which work within a four-pin diamond.

Note that the scale of the exercises in this chapter (and for most of the rest of the book) is reduced for slightly finer thread.

First Spider and Diamond Insertion

In this insertion the centre spiders are replaced by cloth or half stitch diamonds. The cloth stitch diamond with the centre hole is a variation often found in Scandinavian laces, where they are usually worked without the central pins. The ground stitches are the same as for the bookmark.

The insertion needs sixteen pairs of bobbins, wound fully with thread of one colour only, and coupled. (Any excess thread can be used in later exercises.)

To make the pattern for the insertion follow the steps described for construction of the centre section of the Spiders Bookmark pattern, but mark the central diamonds for cloth or half stitch instead of spiders (diagram 9.1).

For the purpose of learning the techniques you should work the sample as shown in the working diagram (diagram 9.2), but if you later wish to work a useful length it would be better not to use all three diamonds together; in terms of design, that arrangement is rather too much of a good thing. Plain cloth and half stitch diamonds are often used together, but the diamond with the hole is generally used alone, as in the bottom half of the sample in the photograph.

You will see from the working diagram that the insertion is not started in a straight line across the top of the

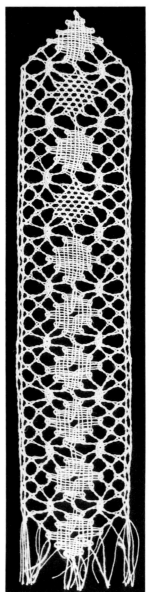

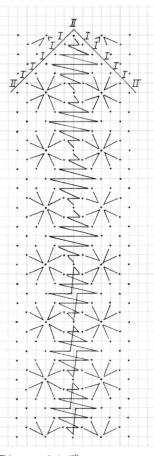

Diagram 9.1 *The pattern diagram for the first insertion. Extend to required length*

Plate 9.1 *The First Spider and Diamond Insertion*

pricking; to do so would involve starting half way through two spiders. It is easier to start at the top of the cloth stitch diamond and bring in new pairs along both diagonals from this point out to the edges, using the spare holes at the top of the pricking for support pins, as indicated by the arrows. (Be sure to remove the support pins once they have served their purpose.)

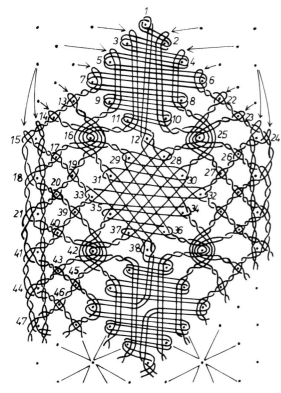

Diagram 9.2 *Working diagram for the first insertion. Note that the sequence of diamond differs from that of the photographed sample. Aesthetically it would not be a good idea to have all three kinds of diamond in the one design*

Begin with two pairs on pin 1, arranged exactly as for pin 1 of the Spiders Bookmark; enclose the pin with cloth stitch and, taking the right hand pair as the worker pair for the diamond, cloth stitch back and forth through pins 2 to 12, bringing in new pairs at pins 2 to 7, and leaving a pair out at each of pins 6 to 11. (The pairs left out should each have two twists.) You will then be left with two pairs at pin 12 with which to begin the next diamond. Do not forget the twist on the diamond working pair each time it passes around the pin. After pin 12 resume bringing in new pairs at 13, 14 and 15; hang these pairs on their support pins (one pair for each of 13 and 14, and two for 15) and work the stitches in the normal way, making ground stitches at 13 and 14 and starting the Torchon edge at 15. You may then work the spider at 16, followed by pins 17 to 21. Next bring in the remaining new pairs at 22, 23 and 24 as for 13, 14 and 15, and continue on, carefully following the numbered order in the working diagram. Notice that the bottom pin of each diamond is enclosed with whatever stitch is used in the following diamond.

When you come to the third diamond variation the central hole is made half way across the sixth row by leaving the workers hanging as passives next to the middle pair of passives (originally from the top pin of the diamond), which then take over as workers for the rest of the diamond. You may use pins to support the pairs at the hole, but with a little more experience you will not need such aids.

The working order suggested, for this and all other exercises in the book, is clearly not the only way that the work might proceed. As you become more experienced other ways will occur to you which are just as efficient, and which you may prefer; as long as you are methodical and understand what you are doing, you may work in any order you wish, within the limits of the design.

You will notice in this insertion that the right hand pair of threads was consistently taken as the working pair (to the right) after the top pin of each diamond was enclosed. It would have been equally correct always to take the left hand pair as workers. The important thing is to be consistent within the one piece of lace as inconsistencies are surprisingly noticeable.

Second Spider and Diamond Insertion

Again this insertion is based on the bookmark pattern, but with cloth or half stitch diamonds on either side of the centre spiders. See plate 9.2, diagram 9.3. It also uses sixteen pairs of bobbins, which should be coupled. To use up the thread from the first insertion tie the threads together in pairs and wind the knot far enough onto one bobbin or the other so that it will not emerge in the sample (about 50 cm or 18"). If you misjudge this and meet a knot pass it

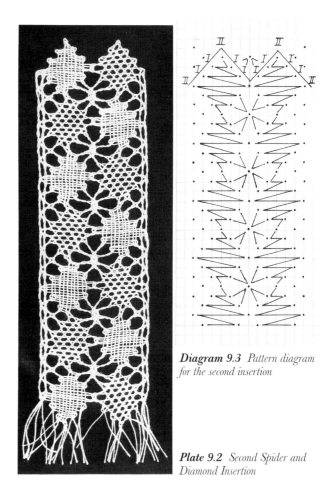

Diagram 9.3 *Pattern diagram for the second insertion*

Plate 9.2 *Second Spider and Diamond Insertion*

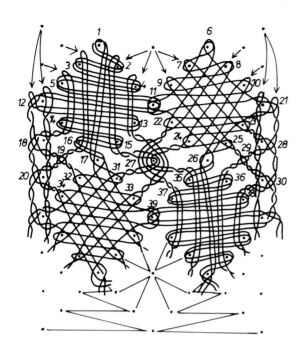

Diagram 9.4 *Working diagram for the second insertion*

away as described at the end of Chapter 2. If the knot is in one of the diamond working threads, see the note on making a faulty stitch, also at the end of Chapter 2.

Allowing for the difference in design the rest of the starting procedure is the same as for the first insertion, but you will notice from diagram 9.4 that the order of the working has had to change considerably. In particular, the workers of the side diamonds meet at a central pin, so neither can proceed beyond this point without the involvement of the other. In a design like this it can sometimes be difficult to find an order of working which moves smoothly as well as being efficient. The only other situation you have not met before occurs where the diamonds meet the Torchon edge; at these points the diamond workers, instead of a ground stitch pair, will be the inner pair of the three involved at the edge pin; the edge pin stitches can then be worked quite normally, excepting that when the edge passives pass through a cloth stitch diamond they should not be twisted.

You will notice that the working pairs of the diamonds on each side of this insertion move in opposite directions, so that they come together at the central pin after working the same row of their respective diamonds. This looks better than if both workers had moved in the same direction. Try it and you will see what I mean.

10 Torchon Fans

Materials:
50/2 or 60/2 linen, or no. 12 Madeira Tanne or equivalent
2.5 mm (10 to the inch) graph paper

The Torchon Fan Sampler

The fan-shaped edging motif is the most common method of shaping the headside of Torchon laces. The two main kinds of Torchon fan are the simple fan and the fish-tail fan and both are included in the sampler, together with their most common variations (see plate 10.1). The first four are simple fans in which the working pair travels back and forth horizontally; the last three are fish-tail fans in which the workers travel diagonally, excepting for the central 'rib' which is worked horizontally. The photograph and working diagrams (diagrams 10.6 and 10.7) show these differences clearly. Both kinds of fan take in passive pairs from the ground along their top edges, and return them to the ground along their lower edges, in the same way as the passives entered and left the diamonds of the Chapter 9 insertions. The ground stitches are again Torchon with two twists, and the footside edge is the standard Torchon edge. (You may vary the ground if you wish.)

CONSTRUCTION OF THE PATTERN FOR THE SIMPLE FANS

In simple Torchon fan patterns, the division between the fans and the ground forms a continuous zigzag line of pin holes, because the fans adjoin each other; the last pin hole of one fan is also the first pin hole of the following fan. Clearly the size of the fans is determined by the number of pin holes along each leg of the zigzag; in this pattern there are five, which means that each fan has nine pin holes along its inner edge if you include the common pin hole. See diagrams 10.1 and 10.2.

Begin by marking in the zigzag line of pin holes down the centre of the pattern space (part a of diagram 10.2). Next mark in the footside edge one pin hole space to the right of the inner points of the fans. Only one repeat of the pattern is shown but you should continue marking until you have four repeats.

Next draw in the curves. There are several ways of doing this. The simplest way is to draw in one curve and

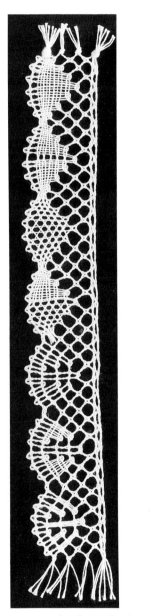

Plate 10.1 *The Torchon Fan Sampler*

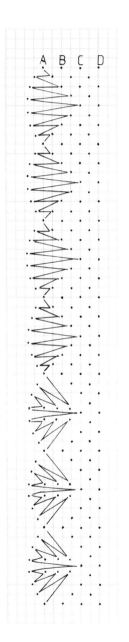

Diagram 10.1 *The pattern diagram for the Torchon Fan Sampler. Stages in the construction of the pattern are described below*

its pin holes, trace off these markings on to a piece of clear acetate film (from a shirt box or some such), then prick through the pinhole markings on the film to make a

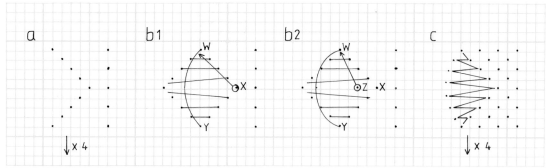

Diagram 10.2 *Stages in the construction of the simple fan pattern*

stencil or template for subsequent curves. Part b of diagram 10.2 shows the method of drawing in the initial curve and its pin holes. First draw in (pencil) guidelines for the pinholes by making the first fan base into a diamond, and ruling in lines as shown. Then draw in the curve either with a circle template, or by using a compass, placing its point on X, the inner point of the fan, and opening it wide enough to draw a curve through the two outer points Y and W (part b1). If you want a deeper curve, simply move the point of the compass one or more graph paper intersections to the left (Z in part b2)

For any fan there must always be an even number of pins along the curve, and for a simple fan it will always be one less than the total number along its two inner edges, so that there will be an even number of rows in the completed fan. This in turn is necessary to ensure that the fan workers finish in the correct position to begin the next fan, that is, to the left of the common pin. If a fan had an uneven number of rows this would not happen. Part c of diagram 10.2 shows a completed pattern repeat, with all remaining (ground) pin holes marked and a zigzag line tracing the passage of the fan worker pair. (The pencil guidelines have been erased.)

CONSTRUCTION OF THE PATTERN FOR THE FISH-TAIL FANS

The outer curve and its pin holes are arrived at in the same way for fish-tail fans as for simple fans, but in other respects the construction is different (diagram 10.3). Both kinds of fans are included on the one sampler, so that the differences can be more readily appreciated. Firstly, when defining the outline of the fans only the extreme points of

the zigzag are marked; the intervening three points are ignored because the stitches worked along this line do not use pins (part a of diagram 10.3). The other main difference is the provision of a double row of pin holes across the middle of the fans; part b of diagram 10.3 shows how these are positioned. The concentric arcs coincide with the passage of the fan passives. Part c is one repeat of the completed pattern. When you have worked the sampler you will readily appreciate the greater efficiency of the fish-tail fan section, producing as it does the same width of lace as in the first section, but with fewer threads and therefore fewer stitches.

The method described in this chapter for marking in the pin holes along the curve will only work for fish-tail fans if there are as many pin holes along each side of the rib as there are passives in the fan. This will vary according to the whim of the designer, and may mean that you will have to space the curve pin holes by eye or measure them off with a ruler. The exercises in Chapter 13 illustrate this.

Calculating the number of pairs needed for the simple fan pattern follows the same rule as observed in earlier exercises; that is, allow two pairs for each pin hole, or pin hole position, across the width of the pattern plus an extra pair for the footside passives.

Counting the pairs needed for a fish-tail fan pattern varies slightly from this rule in that one counts the pin hole positions across the narrowest part of the pattern, instead of the widest part (remember, you discarded two pairs before working this section of the sampler).

It is important to observe that it is not necessary for every pin hole to be marked in before you make the calcu-

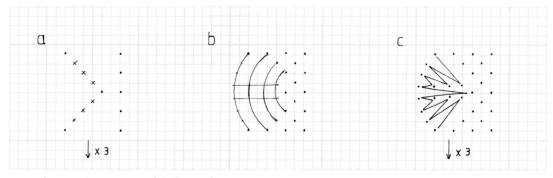

Diagram 10.3 *Stages in the construction of the fish-tail fan pattern*

lation; you only need to know the width of the pattern and the size of the grid so that you can count the number of intersections where pin holes would be marked for a standard Torchon mesh. In fact, very few patterns will ever have a complete horizontal line of pins to be conveniently counted, because elements of the design will interrupt the mesh; for example, a cloth stitch diamond only has pins round its edges, but it would be a great mistake to leave out of your calculation the pairs needed to fill the space inside the diamond.

Working the Torchon Fan Sampler

Make the pricking for the sampler from the pattern diagram (diagram 10.1) in the usual way. You will need eleven pairs of bobbins wound with thread of one colour only. (You should have thread left over from the previous exercises.) As this is a sampler the pairs may be knotted around their starting pins to save time. The photograph shows them knotted and the working diagram (diagram 10.6) shows them coupled, should you wish to take the extra trouble that this would entail.

As the techniques you are learning get more complex verbal explanation becomes more clumsy. The instruction therefore relies more heavily on diagrams and less on words for this and subsequent exercises. This should not be a problem to you at this stage but you will have to pay very careful attention to the fine details of the working diagrams.

Four pairs start at A, two at each of B and C, and three at D. For a knotted start arrange the pairs as in diagram 10.4, with a single overhand knot at each pin. For a coupled start arrange the pairs as in diagram 10.5. It is never sufficient just to hang ground stitch pairs over the pin; they must be interlocked or the starting loops will separate once the pin is removed. The pairs on pin A will

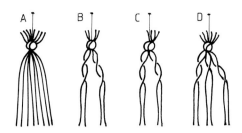

Diagram 10.4 *The pairs knotted ready to start the fan sample*

all stay in the fan; the outer left pair is the fan worker pair and the other three are the edge passives which will be used to fill the curve. (Only two pairs would be needed at A if there was no curve.) The pairs on B, C and D begin as ground stitch pairs but, with the exception of the edge passives, all eventually take a turn as passives in the fans.

Pin A: hang four pairs in order around the pin. The first pair on the left will be the fan workers.

Pins B and C: hang two pairs on the pin, one inside the other. One bobbin of each pair now lies on either side of the pin, forming pairs in a different way; twist one of these pairs only (it does not matter which) and enclose the pin with a half stitch, followed by an extra twist on both pairs.

Pin D: start two pairs as for pins B and C, but leaving the right hand pair, only, with an extra twist; hang another pair around the same pin to the left of the other two, and work it with the nearest pair in cloth-and-twist, leaving the pair now on the left with an extra twist. The pair now in the middle will be the edge passive pair, which may be lifted off the pin and gently pulled down into position once the first few ground stitches have been worked.

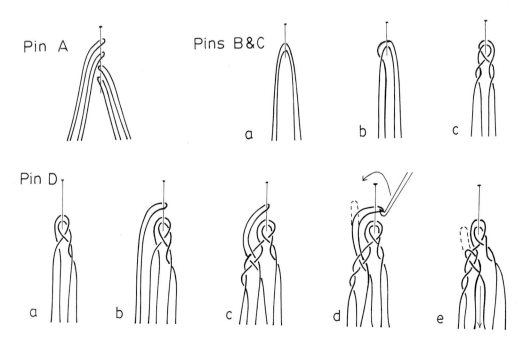

Diagram 10.5 *Arranging the pairs on the pricking for a coupled start*

In most fan patterns the order of working reduces very efficiently to a diagonal band of ground stitches (as wide as is necessary to provide the pairs for the fan), followed by the complete fan, followed by the next diagonal band of ground stitches, and so on. Because this particular pattern is rather narrow the diagonal band is more like a triangle, and the first triangle is incomplete because the start was arranged in a straight line across the pricking; nevertheless the same principle applies, so having arranged the pairs around the starting pins, first work the ground stitch pins 1 to 5.

Working the simple fans

When you have worked the ground stitch pins to pin 5 there will be sufficient ground stitch pairs free to complete the first fan through pins 6 to 19. This fan is worked in cloth stitch with cloth-and-twist edge (first sampler, section 3) and the outer left pair is taken as the worker pair (diagram 10.6). Work back and forth bringing a pair in from the ground at each of the pins 6, 8, 10 and 12, and leaving a pair out after 12, 14, 16 and 18. After pin 19 (and its equivalent in subsequent fans) you should work the first row of the next fan, to the right through the three edge passives only, leaving the workers ready to work pin 34 when the appropriate ground stitch pair is available. Next work the ground stitch triangle pins 34 to 47. This fan is also worked in cloth stitch with cloth-and-twist on the outer edge, but with the extra decoration of a twist on all the passive pairs between the middle two rows. The second fan finishes at pin 47 and the third fan is worked in half stitch with cloth-and-twist on the outer edge.

When changing from cloth stitch to half stitch you will improve the appearance of the transition if you twist all the passives before working the first row of half stitch. This means that after pin 47 you will need to twist the second and third edge passives (the first pair will be twisted as part of the edge stitch) before working the first row of the half stitch fan across to, but not yet including, pin 62. A similar thing must happen in the middle of the fourth fan; after working the row of cloth stitch from W to X the fan passives should all be twisted before working the first row of half stitch from X to Y.

If you do not make these extra twists before the half stitch there will appear to be more rows of cloth stitch than half stitch in the fan. If you need to be convinced try it and see. On your first sampler I did not bother you with this refinement because it was not relevant in the context of a sampler of basic stitches; in fact, it is only really applicable when dividing in half a shape in which there is an even number of rows. (More about this later.) You will also notice in the fourth fan that the cloth-and-twist edge of the cloth stitch section looks better if the twist on the working pair is omitted before and after the edge stitches. Otherwise the edge will appear too open to contrast effectively with the half stitch. When the fourth fan is completed work the next triangle of ground stitches and you will then be ready to work the first of the three fish-tail fans, for which

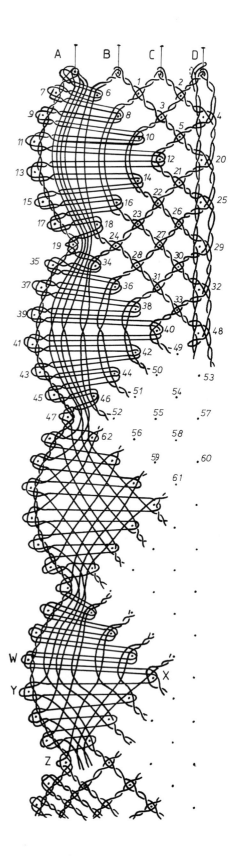

Diagram 10.6 *The working diagram for the simple fans*

the pattern of working is entirely different from that of the simple fans.

Working the fish-tail fans

In working the fish-tail fans (diagram 10.7), you will have no further use for the two extra edge passive pairs, that is, the second and third passive pairs from the left. In the diagram they are shown cut off but at this stage it is better to hang them back over the completed work to be cut off later. The outermost passive pair and the fan workers continue into the next fans. You will also notice that there is no row of pins to define the inner edge of the fan, and only its central rib is worked horizontally (two rows, f to g and g to h); in the rest of the fan the workers travel in diagonal rows towards and away from the central rib. The passive pairs pass through the fan in parallel curves, being held in place by the pins above and below the rib. As you would expect, with fewer pairs to fill the same space, the effect of the fish-tail fans is much lighter. In the first of these fans the stitches are all cloth-and-twist, with an extra twist on the worker pair only, between each stitch. The working diagram shows this clearly. Follow the lettered order of working through pins a to n, turning your pillow as necessary to facilitate working the diagonal rows of the fan.

Fans 6 and 7 follow exactly the same principle of working but the arrangement of stitches is different. The sixth fan has the same cloth-and-twist edge and rib as the fifth, but the rest is worked in cloth stitch. The last fan has the same edge as the first two; the remainder is in cloth stitch, with twists on the passive pairs, only, in each alternate row.

Examine diagram 10.1 and plate 10.1 carefully for the exact pattern of stitches. (Note that the pairs entering and leaving the ground stitch areas must have the twists appropriate to whatever ground stitch is being used. I have used Torchon with two twists, but you may have decided differently.) When you have completed the last fan and the last few ground stitches, finish off in the usual way.

These two kinds of fan are very typical of Torchon lace, and you may find even more variations than those presented here. The principle of working them will be the same, but you should cultivate the habit of examining the lace, or its photograph, very carefully for details.

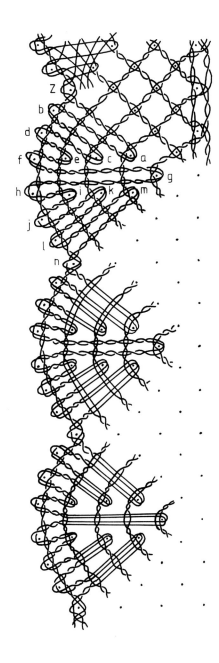

Diagram 10.7 *The working diagram for the fish-tail fans*

11 Turning Corners and Joining Up

Materials:
50/2 or 60/2 linen, or no. 12 Madeira Tanne or equivalent
2.5 mm (10 to the inch) graph paper

The Square Edging

This next exercise is quite a milestone in your lacemaking. Learning how to turn a corner, and how to join up neatly, opens up all sorts of possibilities, and there is very little involved that you have not met before. The pattern given is for a square edging with the smallest practical number of pattern repeats. If later you wish to work, say, a handkerchief edging, you will need to reduce the size of the grid considerably and add more pattern repeats to each side.

Obviously, the wrong side of the square will be the side with the knots on; that is, the side uppermost as you work, since the joining is done on the pillow. In fact, convention has it that this is the wrong side of any lace, but in Torchon there is no noticeable difference unless the piece has a join.

Plate 11.1 *The Square Edging*

CONSTRUCTION OF THE PATTERN

The first step in making this pattern is to mark out the major construction lines for a length of edging containing the design elements decided upon, namely, simple fans and six-pair spiders. Making a corner in such a pattern is not difficult as each pattern repeat ends along a diagonal which is also appropriate as a break for a corner (diagram 11.1).

Having arrived at such a point in the marking you could turn the corner, keeping intact the continuity of the design, by retaining the last diagonal row of pin holes of the pattern repeat before the corner as the first row of the repeat after the corner. This would give a row of pin holes right on the corner line, which looks very nice on the pattern but is complicated to work, and not really appropriate for a corner with fans. A more satisfactory corner is produced by making a complete break in the design so that there is a row of pin holes on either side of the actual corner line, one being the last row of the repeat before the corner, and the other being the first row of the repeat after the corner. These rows are marked exactly parallel with each other and one grid space apart. Part a of the diagram should clarify this.

Now turn the graph paper through 90° and proceed to mark the pattern for the second side of the square. The second and subsequent corners are made in the same way as the first. Part b of the diagram shows major markings for the completed square, including two extra pins right on the corner line, which are necessary to make a neat turn. To vary the size of the square you would simply vary the number of pattern repeats along each side. Part c is the finished pattern with all markings complete.

In making a corner for any fan pattern the corner break should always be made at the narrowest part of the fan. If this is not suitable for other parts of the design, it is those parts which must be modified, not the fans. Any attempt to turn a corner half way through a fan is bound to look clumsy.

Working the Square Edging

Make the pricking from the pattern diagram and pin it to the centre of your pillow. You will need thirteen pairs of bobbins, all coupled. You will also need a fine crochet hook (0.6 mm if possible) when joining up. If you consider the design you will see that it is not practical to start in a straight line across the pricking because that would involve start-

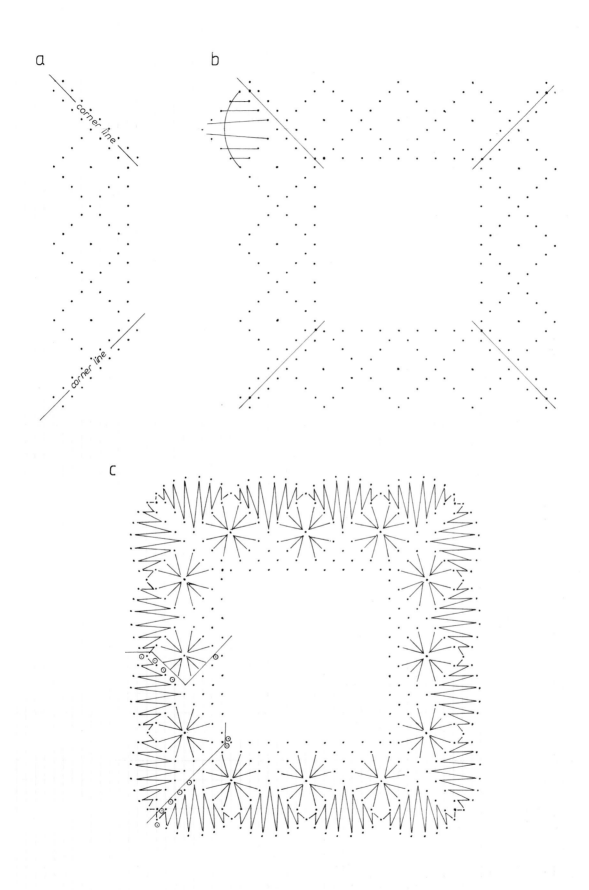

Diagram 11.1 *Stages in the construction of the pattern for the Square Edging. Part c of the diagram is the completed pattern*

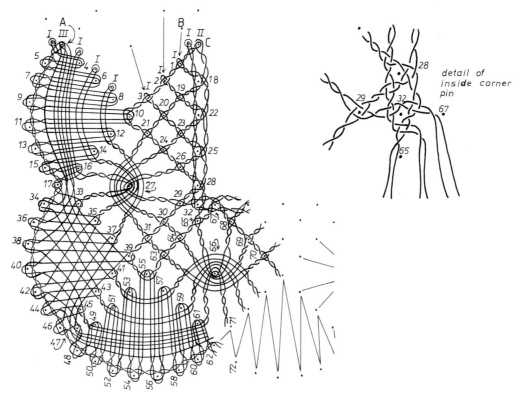

Diagram 11.2 *The working diagram for starting the Square Edging away from the corner*

detail of inside corner pin

ing either half way through a spider, or through the widest part of the fan. Not only would this be awkward but it would also make the join very noticeable. It is much better to start either on a diagonal or in a V shape along a natural division in the pattern. Many lacemakers prefer to use the diagonal corner line for the join, but English lacemakers almost invariably avoid using the corner; it is entirely a matter of personal preference, and both methods are shown, although more prominence is given the English method. You should need no other information to start than that contained in the working diagram (diagram 11.2). If in doubt refer back to the relevant parts of previous exercises. The fans are simple fans, worked alternately in cloth stitch and half stitch, each with a cloth-and-twist edge. The ground stitch shown is Torchon with two twists.

The Roman numerals at the top of the diagram indicate the number of pairs to be started at each point and the arrows point from existing pins in the pattern which may be used as temporary support pins. The circles indicate support pins which should be left in place until the lace is finished. When starting the four pairs at the top of the fan hang the worker pair on the adjacent support pin and arrange the three passive pairs in order around their pin so that when you come to join up your square you will have four separate and identifiable loops to tie off into, once the pin is removed. For the same reason the remaining fan passives, and the footside edge passive pair, are also supported on extra pins until the work is finished.

To make the least conspicuous join possible you must really think about the joining process as you start the work. For example, make sure that you remove any temporary

support pins (those above the starting line) once they have served their purpose, and pull the starting loops down into their correct position. If you forget to do this it will be quite impossible to make a neat join. It is also important that the stitches around the starting pins are consistent with whatever would ordinarily be there; it would be most noticeable, for example, if a starting pin were enclosed with a cloth stitch when the following ground stitch pins are to be enclosed by half stitches. Keeping these points in mind, and following the working diagram very carefully, work through to pin 31 and pause a moment. Pin 32 is an extra pin on the corner line at the point where the footside edge lines would intersect if extended. Its sole purpose is to assist in making a sharp right angle turn at the corner, and it is worked as for any other Torchon edge pin, using the three pairs nearest the edge, but omitting the extra twist on the outermost pair both before and after the pin, because there simply is not room for it.

After pin 32 complete the fan through pins 33 to 46. Pin 47 is another extra pin on the corner line, which allows an extra two (very short) rows to be worked to contain the three edge passives and to manoeuvre the fan workers into the right position to begin the next fan. (Make sure that only the three edge passives pass to the left of this pin.) Once pin 47 has been worked you can turn your pillow through 90° and begin the second side of the square by working the third fan, followed by the second spider and the fourth fan, and so on. When you are about half way along the second side you can begin taking the pins from behind but you should leave in all the pins in the first pattern repeat, say up to pin 39, as well as all the headside and footside edge pins. These should be pushed right into the pillow so that they are not in the way of later work. It is also most important to protect the completed work with a cover cloth.

By the time you have worked all four corners of the square you should have a good understanding of the procedure. After the fourth corner continue working until you meet the starting loops. Note that on the footside edge the pair from B must be worked through the edge passive pair in cloth-and-twist, before either is tied off to complete the triangle of stitches around pin C (the other two stitches were part of the starting procedure). The fan workers must finish up to the left of the three edge passive pairs above pin A. Make sure all the pins above the joining line are pushed into the pillow out of your way.

The footside edge is probably the best place to begin tying off because once this is secured it is easy to establish the correct order for the rest of the tying off (diagram 11.3). First remove pin C to reveal the starting loops of the two interlocked pairs into which the two extreme right hand pairs must be tied. Taking your fine crochet hook, push it through the double loop from the top and hook through the top thread (as it lies twisted) of one of the pairs to be tied off; cut the bobbin off this thread, leaving about 10 cm (4") and pull the cut end right through the loop; then cut off the other bobbin of the pair and push aside these threads until you have repeated the procedure for the second pair of threads to be tied off into this loop. At this point replace the pin in the pricking to the left of the starting loop, not

through it; this is in fact its normal position in relation to the three edge pin stitches. It is now safe to tie off the cut ends in pairs with a reef knot, tensioning them around the pin you have just replaced.

Next remove the support pin and tie off the edge passives into their starting loop; the edge is now quite secure. Then tie off the right hand legs of the spider in turn into the middle of the stitches at pins 1, 2 and 3, removing each of these pins only as you come to it. The remaining three spiders' legs tie off into the starting loops on the support pins near pins 8, 6 and 4. (Remember, you must pull the top thread through the loop, as shown in the first part of diagram 11.3,) or you will lose one of the twists on the finishing thread. At this stage you will be left with only the fan workers and the three edge passives to be tied off.

Following diagram 11.4, first remove the worker support pin to reveal the worker starting loop, and tie off the fan workers into it. Then remove the pin which supports the starting loops of three edge passives, and replace it in its hole with the three loops to its right. Finally, tie off the three passive pairs, in order, into these loops. The tying off process is now complete so you may remove all remaining pins and lift the lace from the pillow.

You will now have a lot of long ends which may be dealt with in a number of ways. For a piece which will not be washed or handled but perhaps mounted under glass, it is simplest just to cut the ends off short. For an article which will be in regular use, a better method is to darn the ends in with a needle and thread, taking each thread of a pair in

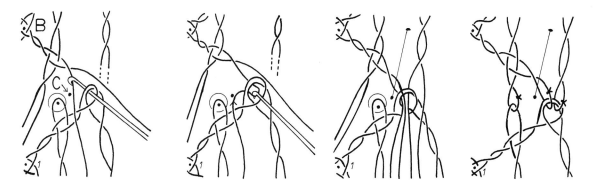

Diagram 11.3 *Tying off the footside edge pairs*

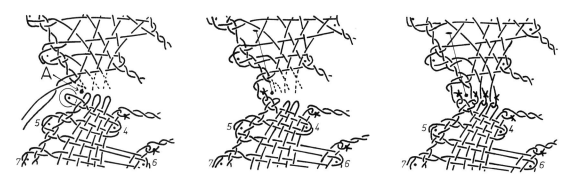

Diagram 11.4 *Stages in tying off the fan workers and the three edge passives*

opposite directions away from the knot. This is certainly the most durable method and with care can be quite inconspicuous, especially if the lace is worked in fine thread. You need not bother to darn in the ends on the footside edge, as these can be hidden in the hem of the fabric the lace is mounted on.

For a lace worked in heavy thread lacemakers often rely only on knots, even for frequently used items, as darning-in is too clumsy. In that case the tying off is done slightly differently. When the top thread of the finishing pair has been hooked through its starting loop the other finishing thread is passed through the hooked loop, both ends are then pulled up and knotted in the usual way (see diagram 11.5). The knot will then be located firmly on the back of the work and will be more secure than a plain reef knot. This method is known as the 'sewings' method because of its similarity to the technique of that name which is used in sectional laces such as Honiton and Brussels to join the various parts of the lace whilst the work is in progress.

In my opinion this is not a really secure way to finish off a piece of lace, despite its popularity. A better method

is shown in plates 11.4–11.7 and described in full in Chapter 19. The finishing methods described in this book are not the only ones in practice, but they are probably the simplest.

Starting and finishing along the corner line
As previously mentioned, it is also possible to start and finish a square along the corner line. Diagram 11.6 shows how this would be done, and plates 11.2–11.4 illustrate the tying off process.

Plate 11.2   *The square edging finished at the corner line*

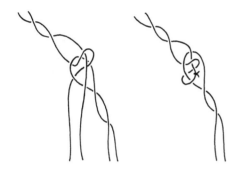

Diagram 11.5 *Tying off by the 'sewings' method*

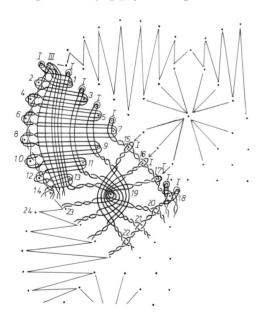

Diagram 11.6 *Working diagram for starting the square edging along the corner line*

Plate 11.3   *Starting with the inside corner pin, one thread of the finishing pair is pulled through the edge starting loop*

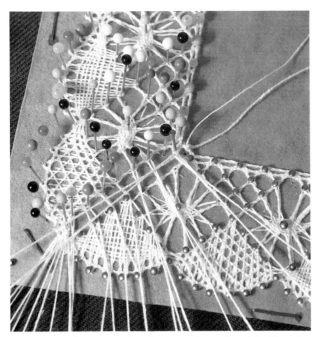

Plate 11.4 *The threads of the finishing pair are then tied off into the starting loop*

Plate 11.6 *Tie off fan pairs into their starting loops*

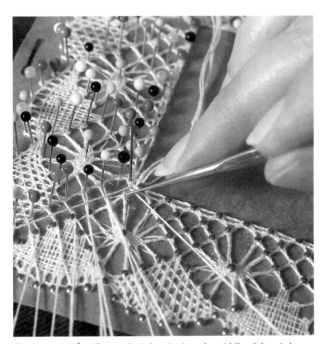

Plate 11.5 *Tie off ground stitch pairs into the middle of the stitch*

Plate 11.7 *The finishing ends oversewn along the tying-off line (see the section on finishing in Chapter 19 for a full description)*

12 Cloth or Half Stitch Chevrons

Materials:
50/2 or 60/2 linen, or no. 12 Madeira Tanne or equivalent
2.5 mm (10 to the inch) graph paper

Cloth or half stitch diamonds are the simplest solid shapes in Torchon lace. Chevrons are not much more complicated, especially if you think of them as diamonds with a piece missing. In fact, providing it can be drawn with diagonal lines, almost any cloth or half stitch shape is possible in Torchon lace. Chapter 18 will give you some other ideas for solid shapes.

CONSTRUCTION OF THE PATTERNS

First Chevron Shape Edging
Chevron shapes, although solid, give a lighter effect than diamonds. This design combines fish-tail fans, four-pair spiders, and cloth or half stitch chevrons. Diagram 12.1 shows the stages in making the pattern. Note that the pin holes are measured off along the curve with a ruler, because there are less of them than there would be for a simple fan of the same size; this in turn is due to there being less rib pin holes than there are fan passives, which was referred to at the end of Chapter 10. The diagonal line indicates a suitable corner line, should you wish to experiment with drawing your own corner pattern.

The second edging pattern is simply a variation of the first with bigger spiders and a slightly different chevron shape.

Working the First Chevron Shape Edging
The first edging needs fifteen pairs of bobbins, coupled. Applying what you have learned in previous exercises, and

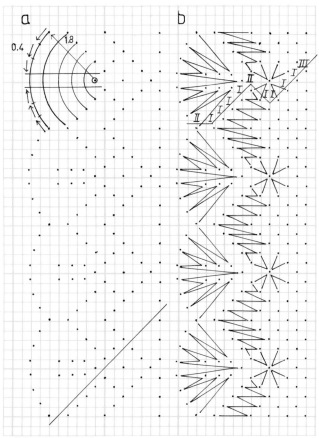

Diagram 12.1 *Stages in constructing the First Chevron Shape Edging pattern. Part b is the completed pattern. Extend it as required*

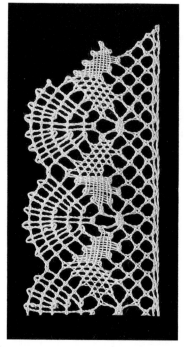

Plate 12.1 *The First Chevron Shape Edging (photograph Sue Stafford)*

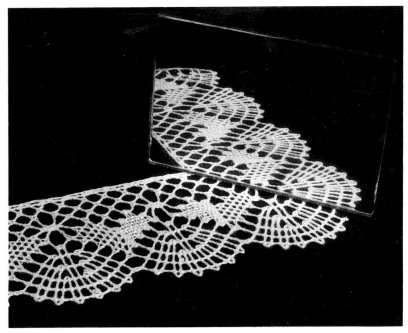

Plate 12.2 *Using a mirror on a length of straight edging to find a pleasing corner break in the pattern*

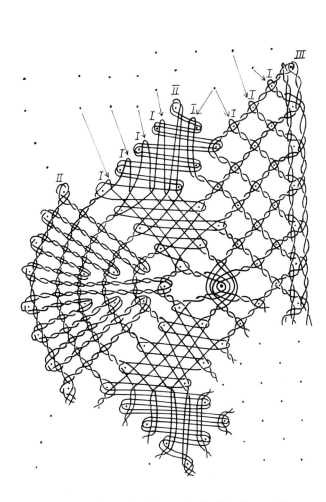

Diagram 12.1 *The working diagram for the First Chevron Shape Edging*

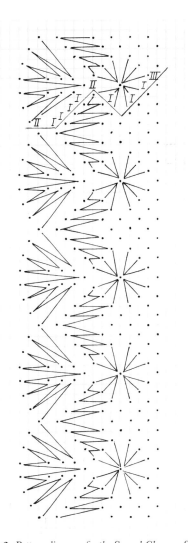

Diagram 12.3 *Pattern diagram for the Second Chevron Shape Edging*

following the working diagram carefully (diagram 12.2), you should be able to start without too much trouble. The fans are the same as the first fish-tail fan in the fan sampler, only slightly bigger. The ground is relieved by a pattern of four-pair spiders, as well as the chevron shapes which are worked half in cloth stitch and half in half stitch. You will notice in these shapes that it is not necessary to twist the passive pairs before the change to half stitch, because there is an odd number of rows in the shape (fifteen to be exact). This is referred to in the notes for working the fourth fan in the fan sampler.

Second Chevron Shape Edging

This edging is a little wider than the first and needs sixteen pairs, again coupled (diagram 12.4). The fans are the same as the last fan on the fan sampler. The spiders are six-pair spiders. The chevron shapes are slightly different from those in the first edging in that the third pin along the inner edge of the shape is left out, resulting in one less row being worked; the space thus made is filled by twisting the passive pairs between the middle rows. Note also that to achieve the correct sequence of rows for these twists it is necessary to take the left hand pair to the left after the top pin in the chevron shape.

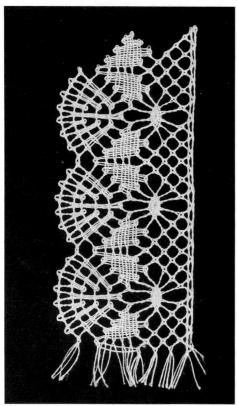

Plate 12.3 *The Second Chevron Shape Edging*

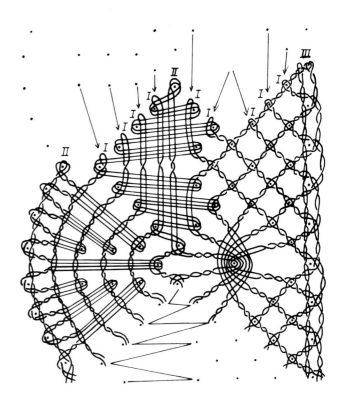

Diagram 12.4 *The working diagram for the Second Chevron Shape Edging*

13 Rose Ground

The Rose Ground Sampler

Materials:
50/2 or 60/2 linen, or no. 12 Madeira Tanne or equivalent
2.5 mm (10 to the inch) graph paper

There are many different versions of this decorative filling
or ground stitch, but the sampler contains just three of the
most common ones. There are also at least two other names
for it—'Point de Marriage'and 'Virgin Ground'. Whatever
it may be called it is the method of working which distin-
guishes rose ground, and that is the same for all versions.

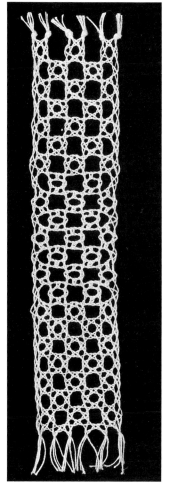

Plate 13.1 *The Rose Ground Sampler*

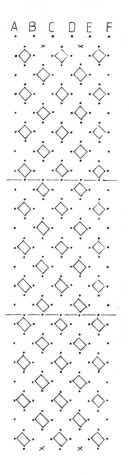

Diagram 13.1 *The pattern diagram for the Rose Ground Sampler*

CONSTRUCTING THE SAMPLER PATTERN
The pattern of pin holes for rose ground is identical with
that of Torchon, and as with Torchon, rose ground is also
worked in diagonal rows. However, as indicated by the
squares on the pattern, each unit ('rose') of rose ground
involves four pin holes, and each row of the ground en-
compasses a double row of pins.

Make the pattern and pricking for the sampler from the
pattern diagram (diagram 13.1). The photograph shows
the sampler worked only in white, but I recommend you
use coloured threads for the pairs in the centre of the sampler, so that you will more readily understand how the
ground is constructed.

Working the Rose Ground Sampler

You will need twelve pairs of bobbins, either knotted
together or coupled (diagram 13.2). Eight of these pairs
should be wound in the main colour, two pairs in one contrasting colour, and two in another colour. For this
sampler it will not matter if you use some of the slightly
heavier coloured thread left over from the earlier exercises.
Two pairs start at each of the pins A to F. For a knotted
start, again use a single knot at each pin; for a coupled
start refer to the start of the fan sampler (pins B and C).

As I mentioned previously, each unit of rose ground
involves four pins. There are, however, six stitches for each
unit as two of them are worked without pins. I have numbered each unit or rose with a Roman numeral to indicate
the order of working, and within each rose the stitches are
numbered 1 to 6. Four pairs of threads are used in each
rose, and rose I begins the sampler with the pairs on A and
B. With the centre two of these pairs work half stitch, pin,
half stitch at 1; with the two pairs now on the left work
half stitch, pin, half stitch at 2; with the two pairs now on
the right work half stitch, pin, half stitch at 3; then with the
two pairs now in the centre work half stitch, pin, half stitch
at 4. Stitches 5 and 6 of every rose are normally worked
without pins, and in the first section of the sampler they
are worked cloth-and-twist. However, when either of these
extra (blind) stitches occurs on an edge it needs a pin to
stabilise it, so stitch 5 of rose I is worked half stitch, pin,
half stitch as for the main pins. The appearance of rose I at
this stage is shown in part a of the working diagram.

Begin the next diagonal row by working rose II with

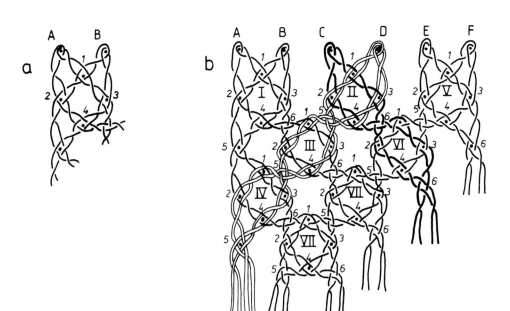
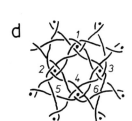

Diagram 13.2 *The working diagram for the Rose Ground Sampler*

the pairs on C and D, in the same way as for I, but observing that no pins are necessary for either 5 or 6. Do not be concerned about the large gaps between the roses at the top of the sampler. These occur because two pins (marked with crosses in diagram 13.1) have been left out of the normal rose ground pattern to make the starting easier; the same thing has been done at the bottom of the sampler. Continue the first section of the sampler down to the first horizontal line. You should have a similar colour pattern to that in the first section of your Torchon sampler.

In the second section of rose ground pins 1 to 4 of each rose are worked cloth-and-twist, pin, cloth-and-twist (part c of the diagram). The blind stitches are the same as in the first section. The contrast threads will make a band down the centre of the sampler, similar to the second section of the Torchon sampler.

In the third section of rose ground pins 1 to 4 are worked as in Section 1, but the blind stitches are half stitches (d). The colour pattern will be similar to Section 1.

Rose ground is a very popular stitch in Torchon lace, and is often used in place of the Torchon grounds. It also occurs as a filling stitch for a motif within a design, using either a single rose or a group of them.

Some observations about rose ground

As I have already pointed out, the basic pattern of pin holes for rose ground is identical to that of the Torchon ground stitches. It is how those pin holes are used which creates the different stitch, and a few observations about this are necessary to enable you to make use of the rose ground in designing a piece of lace and constructing a pattern for it.

In the rose ground sampler you saw that each row of rose ground was worked along a double row of pin holes. Furthermore, each single rose along a row was worked around four pins, but you were taught to think of it as

having six stitches, as the stitches 5 and 6 in each rose were worked without pins. In fact it is these blind stitches which create the unique structure of rose ground.

The six-step approach is appropriate in a sampler composed entirely of rose ground, but it is not the whole story if you wish to use rose ground as a filling stitch for a motif within a piece of lace, or as a background stitch in conjunction with other motifs. If you consider a single unit of rose ground in isolation you will see that the blind stitches before the central rose are as important as those after it; that is, for a unit of rose ground used alone there are eight stitches, not six. Diagram 13.3 shows this clearly, and also shows the pattern of pin holes which must surround such a single unit to provide the necessary four pairs to work the central rose, namely a diamond with four pins along each side.

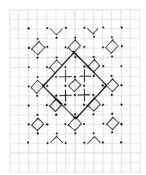

Diagram 13.3 *A single unit of rose ground isolated within the Rose Ground Sampler, showing how the four pairs involved relate to the rest of the ground*

A similar observation may be made of larger diamonds of rose ground; that is, the pattern must always allow for the blind stitches of the pairs entering the roses along the top edges of the diamond. Diagram 13.4 shows both a four-rose and a nine-rose motif. The former has six pins along each of its outer edges, and the latter has eight. (In fact any diamond shaped motif of rose ground will be found to have an even number of pin holes along each of its surrounding edges.)

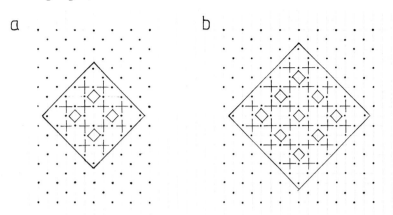

Diagram 13.4 *A four-rose motif and a nine-rose motif*

The use of rose ground is not, of course, restricted to diamond shapes or background stitches. Diagram 13.5 shows a diagonal band of rose ground and also a continuous trail. (You will learn more about trails in Chapter 17.)

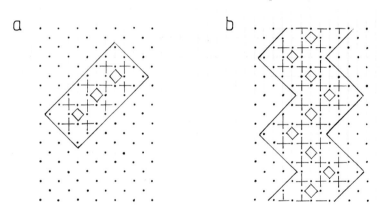

Diagram 13.5 *A diagonal band of rose ground (a) and a continuous trail (b)*

14 Using Gimp Threads

Materials:
50/2 or 60/2 linen, or no. 12 Madeira Tanne or equivalent
2.5 mm (10 to the inch) graph paper

In lacemaking a gimp thread is a heavy outlining thread used to give emphasis to certain parts of a design. Historically, a gimp thread was constructed in a particular way, as hand spinners will be aware, and was often metallic, with a cotton or linen core. Tailors still use a properly constructed gimp thread for cording buttonholes, but in lacemaking it merely means any heavy thread suitable for the purpose.

Insertion with Rose Ground and Gimp Threads

This insertion looks very attractive mounted on table linen of a dark colour, or used as a braid on clothing. There is really nothing new in it, excepting for the gimp thread outlining the diamonds and the edges, which are 'straight headings' rather than the footside edges you have previously worked on insertions. The straight heading or headside is often used in modern laces and is particularly well suited to lace which will be sewn on top of a fabric, rather than set into it.

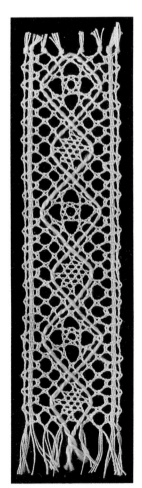

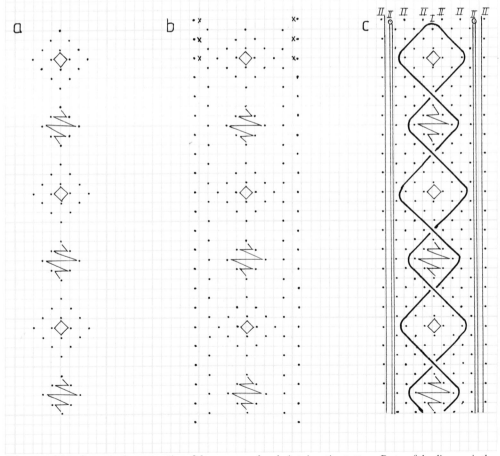

Diagram 14.1 *Stages in the construction of the rose ground and gimp insertion pattern. Part c of the diagram is the completed pattern. Notice how the edge pins are spaced out further than normal to accommodate the three edge passive pairs. The crosses in part b of the diagram indicate the position of the edge pins for the standard Torchon edge*

Plate 14.1 *The Rose Ground and Gimp Insertion*

CONSTRUCTION OF THE PATTERN

Make the pattern for the edging following the steps shown in diagram 14.1.

Working the Rose Ground and Gimp Insertion

You will need sixteen pairs of bobbins, wound with the standard thread, and an extra pair of bobbins wound with a heavy thread such as knitting cotton, six strands of embroidery thread, no. 5 perle cotton, or whatever else you might have on hand which would serve as a gimp thread. For the sampler you will only need about half a metre of gimp on each bobbin.

Make the pricking from the pattern diagram, and attach it to the pillow. Knot or couple two pairs on each of the top pins, including the support pins for the edge passives which are marked by circles. The ground stitches are the standard Torchon with two twists. The edges are in effect narrow braids joined to the rest of the lace at the pins on their inner edges. The edge braids have three passive pairs, and one constant worker pair, and are worked in cloth stitch, with cloth-and-twist on the outer edges.

Guided by the working diagram 14.2, first work the pins 1 to 6 on the left side of the pricking, and pins 7 to 12 on the right hand side. On each side return the braid workers through the passives, and leave them ready to work the next inside edge pin when appropriate. (Remember the previous comments on efficient methods of working.) Notice that whenever the edge braid workers meet a ground stitch pair they are first twisted, then worked cloth-and-twist, pin, cloth-and-twist.

Next hang the gimp pair on a support pin between the middle two pins at the top of the pricking. One gimp thread must now pass to the left through four ground stitch pairs, and the other to the right through four pairs; these pairs should lie ready with one twist only on each pair. If you look carefully at the working diagram you will see that each pair supporting a gimp thread has one twist before the gimp, one around it, and one after it, making three twists in all. To pass the gimp to the left weave it under the first thread of the ground stitch pair and over the second, then twist the pair twice. To pass the gimp to the right pass it over the first thread and under the second, then twist twice. Part b of the diagram should make this clear, but you will find the sequence easy to remember if you observe that whether you are taking the gimp to the left or to the right, you must pass it through the supporting pair in such a way as to lock in the twist that the pair started with.

With the gimp pair in position you should now complete the ground stitches immediately below it, through pins 13 to 19. Then you will have the four pairs necessary to work the rose in the centre of the diamond through pins 20 to 23, making sure that you not only remember the blind stitches after the rose, but also those before it. These are marked with small arrows on the working diagram to remind you. (In the rose ground sampler these stitches occurred automatically as part of previous roses.) When the rose ground motif is completed work the ground stitches 24 to 28, then turn the gimp threads towards the centre of the work and pass each through four pairs. When they meet they may be either crossed or twisted; whichever method you choose you must be consistent throughout, because it will be very noticeable if you are not. The rest of the insertion should be quite straightforward as you have worked half stitch diamonds before.

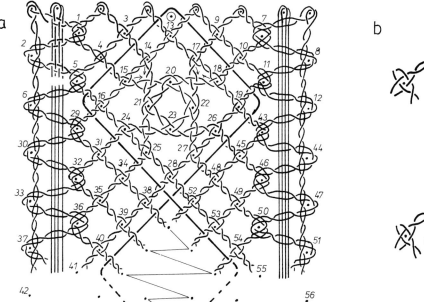

Diagram 14.2 *(a) General working diagram for the Rose Ground and Gimp Insertion; (b) Passing the gimp thread through ground stitch pairs*

15 Scallops and Points

Materials:
50/2 or 60/2 linen, or no. 12 Madeira Tanne or equivalent
2.5 mm (10 to the inch) graph paper

Rose Ground and Scallops Edging

This exercise has been designed to show you how the Torchon edge is worked with rose ground and to introduce you to a headside with scallops (or points) rather than fans. The visual effect of these is to give more emphasis to the ground stitch, whereas in a fan edging it is the fans which generally have more impact.

Both points and scallops are easily included in the one sampler (plate 15.1) because there is no difference in the manner of their working, and both require the same number of pairs. It must be said, however, that points are more difficult to work neatly, especially in cloth stitch, and if you wish to extend this exercise to make a border for a mat it would look better if you chose one or the other edge finish.

CONSTRUCTION OF THE PATTERN

Both scallops and fan patterns have a zigzag division between ground and headside, which creates the need to carry the threads left out of the ground along each decrease edge of the zigzag until they need to be taken in again along the adjacent increase edge. However, in the case of fan edgings, the headside curves outwards *between* each peak of the zigzag, and with scallops it curves *around* each peak. The pointed headside is merely a variation on this, which follows the line of the ground stitches more closely. In both scalloped and pointed edges the headside forms a continuous trail which varies in density according to the number of pairs being carried.

Diagram 15.1 show the stages in making the pattern for the edging. Begin by marking out the adjoining triangles of rose ground roses (each with a common rose) to give a straight footside edge on the right, and a zigzag outline on the left. The line of pin holes dividing headside and ground can then be added, one grid space to the left of the roses, to allow for the blind stitches. The headside edge is then marked in relation to this dividing line. Part b of the diagram shows the guide lines for both the curved headside

and the headside with points. At the widest part of the pattern the headside of both versions is one grid space wide. Part c of the diagram shows the finished pattern of pin holes and all other appropriate markings. Note that there are the same numbers of pin holes on both sides of the headside trail, and that they are horizontally opposite each other. Finally, as with previous exercises, the number of pin holes across the widest part of the pattern is used to calculate the number of pairs of threads necessary; that is, the number of pins multiplied by two, plus one pair of footside passives.

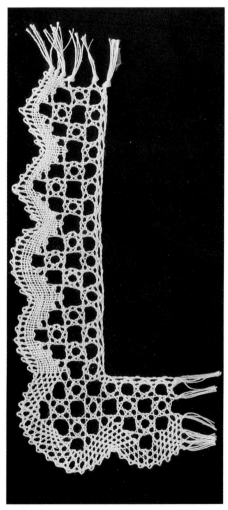

Plate 15.1 *The Rose Ground and Scallops Edging*

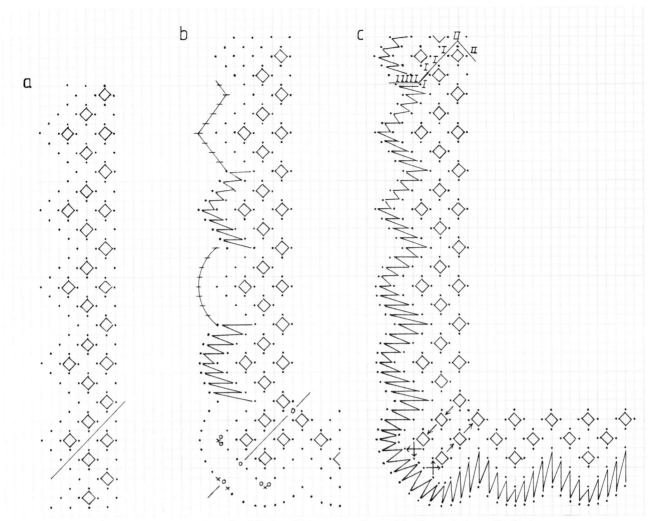

Diagram 15.1 *Stages in making the Rose Ground and Scallops Edging pattern. Part c of the diagram is the completed pattern*

The bottom of part b of the diagram shows the basis of the corner for the edging pattern. Note that a re-arrangement of pins is necessary in the headside trail, on either side of the corner line, to keep the angle of working correct. The crosses indicate pin holes removed and the circles indicate extra pin holes added.

Working the Rose Ground and Scallops Edging

This edging needs thirteen pairs of bobbins, and they should be coupled, as it is simpler to start the pattern along a diagonal (although the photograph shows the pairs knotted and a straight start). Make the pricking from the pattern diagram and begin the sample along the first complete diagonal of the pricking. Use the diagonal above for support pins as needed (diagram 15.2).

As verbal explanation of every detail of the start of this pattern would be very lengthy, I suggest that before you begin working you examine the working diagram very carefully, mentally following every stitch. Then, when you start, only hang on the new pairs as you need them. Take care not to miss out the blind stitches between each rose as they are not numbered. Notice that there is a row of extra

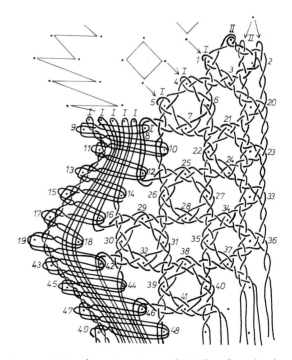

Diagram 15.2 *The working diagram for the Rose Ground and Scallops Edging*

pin holes at the start of the headside to indicate support pins for all but one of the headside passives; this remaining one is taken in from the ground after the first diagonal row of rose ground has been worked, and it enters the headside at the pin from which the headside workers start. When you pin the worker pair into position you must therefore take care that the pair from the ground passes behind the pin to lie to the left of it, before you start working the row across to pin 9. The footside edge pins are worked exactly as for a normal Torchon edge. The only thing to observe is that the edge stitches make it unnecessary to work the blind stitches entering and leaving the right hand side of the edge roses.

If you follow the diagram and photograph carefully, the rest of the sample should be fairly straightforward. Be careful to work all the extra pin holes on the inside of the corner scallop to keep the headside workers travelling at the right angle.

Once you have turned the pillow at the corner, the order of working always appears to proceed from the headside down to the footside, but in fact it follows the normal order (footside down to headside) if you imagine the footside line extended above the corner point. It only appears to be different because all the diagonal rows in the section immediately following the corner line are incomplete, until you reach the one which begins at the inside corner point. This applies to all patterns with a corner, but small details of the working will vary according to the design of the lace.

Square Mat with a Gimp

This small mat (plate 15.2) is derived from the scalloped edge pattern and has an edging which is mid-way between points and scallops. The centre design is made with a single gimp thread. The ground stitches are Torchon with two twists, and the headside is worked in half stitch, with cloth-and-twist at the outer edge. The mat may also be worked with rose ground in place of the gimp design.

CONSTRUCTION OF THE PATTERN
Make the pattern for the mat following the steps in diagram 15.3.

Plate 15.2 *The Square Mat*

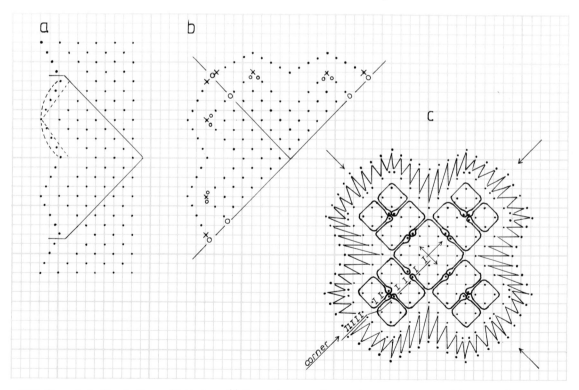

Diagram 15.3 *Stages in drafting the Square Mat pattern: (a) Converging corner lines mark a quarter segment of the mat on the edging pattern; the dotted lines show the position of the scallops and points on the original edging; (b) Two segments of the mat with the correct pin sequence; crosses indicate pins left out, and circles indicate pins added; (c) The completed pattern*

Working the Square Mat

Make the pricking from the pattern diagram, and wind twelve pairs of bobbins, coupled, and one gimp bobbin. Study the working diagram carefully and start the pairs as indicated (diagram 15.4). Make sure you leave the headside passive support pins in place so you can tie off more easily into these starting loops when you have finished the mat.

Note that when the gimp thread doubles back on itself it passes through the same twist in the enclosing pair, ex-cepting where it loops around a pin; in that instance the enclosing pair must be twisted before the gimp returns, otherwise it will not be properly enmeshed in the ground stitches.

When you have finished working, both the starting and finishing ends of the gimp must be enclosed in twists be-fore tying off into pins 10 and 12. The rest of the tying off is similar to that of the Square Edging, excepting that the mat does not have a footside.

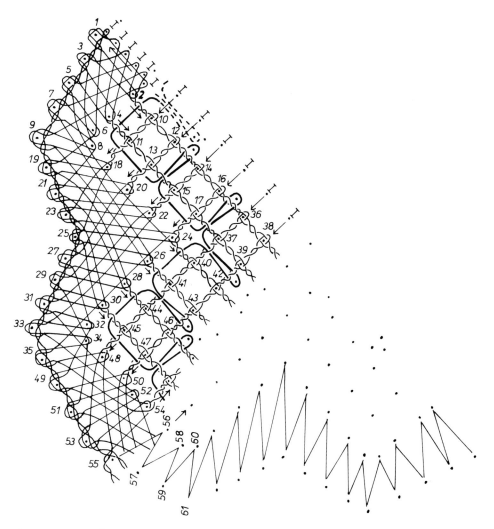

Diagram 15.4 *The working diagram for the Square Mat*

16 Tallies and Leaves

Materials:

35/2 or 40/2 linen or no. 12 cotton perle (for the sampler only)

50/2 or 60/2 linen, or no. 12 Madeira Tanne or equivalent

2.5 mm (10 to the inch) graph paper

Tallies and Leaves Sampler

In Torchon lace the only exception to the basic cross-twist rule is found in the working of tallies and leaves. Two pairs of threads are involved, as in other stitches, but in both leaves and tallies one thread only does all the work, weaving over and under the other three. The result is a tiny patch of weaving in which the three passive (warp) threads are hidden. As beginners often find this procedure difficult I recommend that you practise on the sampler before working them within a piece of lace.

Make the pattern and pricking from diagram 16.1. You will need four pairs of bobbins wound with the heavier thread of earlier exercises. Hang two pairs on pin A and two pairs on B.

Most books on lacemaking stop short of detailed instruction for making tallies or leaves, hoping that readers will either devise their own method or find someone to show them how it is done. I quite understand why this is so as it is very hard to write an adequate description. The method given here is only one of a number of possibilities. You may be able to think of a better way, or a way which is easier for you. The only important consideration is the quality of the work you produce.

Section 1: Tallies

As you will not be needing the outermost pairs until the first tally is completed twist them twice and push them well aside to make plenty of working room. The two middle pairs now make the first tally. Twist each of these once and make the cross movement, followed by a twist on the right hand pair only; then pin at 1 between the two pairs, as in part a of diagram 16.2. (Pin 1 is a support pin only, to assist you in keeping the three warp threads parallel; when you become more proficient you will probably dispense with such an aid.) The outer right hand thread of

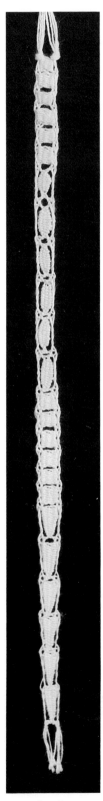

Plate 16.1 *The Tallies and Leaves Sampler*

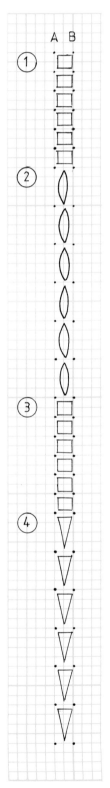

Diagram 16.1 *The pattern diagram for the Tallies and Leaves Sampler*

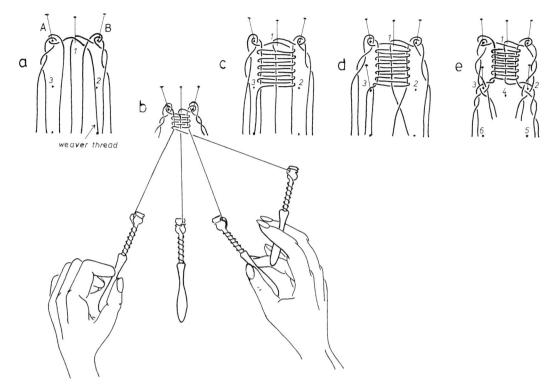

Diagram 16.2 *Stages in making a tally*

these two pairs now becomes the weaver thread and should be lengthened by a generous amount; the three passive threads may be left short, but should be spread out so that their bobbins lie about 5 cm (2") apart.

Now pick up the weaver bobbin and pass it back and forth from right hand to left hand, weaving it over and under the passive threads as you do so. Try to keep the edges of the weaving parallel and neat. When you have woven several rows, tension the work as shown in part b of the diagram. By pulling gently outwards on the outer passive thread, whilst keeping the weaver thread taut, you will be able to slide the rows of weaving up the passive threads so that they are packed more tightly together, without pulling the tally out of shape. Continue weaving and tensioning in this way until you have made about six or eight passes (across and back once makes one pass) and finish with the weaver thread on the left, as in part c of the diagram.

Make a pair of the weaver and its adjacent passive thread, twist this pair once, and pin between its threads at 3, as in part d of the diagram. This is a temporary measure only, to prevent the tally being pulled out of shape whilst you are securing its other side. To do this, twist the remaining pair of passives once and with this pair and the pair laid aside at B make a half stitch, pin, half stitch at 2. Return to the left hand side and make a half stitch with the pair of threads around pin 3 and the pair laid aside at A; remove pin 3 and replace it in the same hole but between the pairs, then enclose the pin with another half stitch (part e of the diagram). The two pairs now on the outside each have one more twist and are laid aside until the next tally is

completed with the two (new) inner pairs.

Make five more tallies by the same method as the first, taking care to make each as neat and square as possible. It is very important not to drop the weaver bobbin at any stage, or to pull it without also keeping tension on the outer passive threads. If by accident you do either of these things you will pull the tally out of shape, and may have to undo it and start again. It is for this reason also that the stitch involving the weaver thread should not be the first stitch made after the tally weaving is completed; if the opposite side of the tally is secured first, it is more likely to hold its shape.

Section 2: Leaves

Diagram 16.3 shows the various stages in making leaves or petals. As you can see, a leaf is a shaped tally which begins and ends in a point. To begin, make a cloth stitch with the two centre pairs, and twist the right hand pair only; the thread now on the right is the weaver thread. Again, you may use a support pin as in part a of the diagram but it is not obligatory. Weave back and forth and tension as for the tally, but allow the rows of weaving to lengthen successively until you judge the leaf to be about two-thirds completed; then begin shaping it in to the bottom point, finishing with the weaver thread on the right (b). Finally, to secure the bottom of the leaf, twist the left hand pair, then make a half stitch with both pairs (c). You may now make the stitches which will exchange the leaf pairs for the pairs laid aside; it is not important which of these you do first as leaves are relatively hard to disturb.

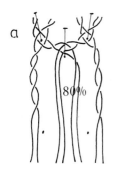 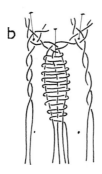 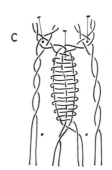 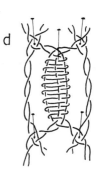

80%

Diagram 16.3 *Stages in making a leaf*

Section 3: Tallies again

As you can see from the photograph this section is a repeat of Section 1. However, I recommend you to finish these tallies on the right so that the first stitch you make after the tally weaving is completed will be the stitch on the left. It is important to be flexible in this matter, for reasons which will emerge in the bookmark sampler.

Section 4: Triangular leaves, or wedge tallies

Triangular leaves begin like tallies and end like leaves.

Tallies and Leaves Bookmark

Although the design may be a little contrived, this sampler has as many arrangements of leaves and tallies as possible in the small space (plate 16.2).

Make the pattern and pricking from the pattern diagram 16.4, in the usual way. As for earlier exercises mark in the main design elements first, then add the ground and borders. Make sure you include the dotted line divisions with the other markings on your pricking.

You will need eighteen pairs of bobbins, coupled. The bookmark has a border similar to the straight heading on the rose ground and gimp insertion, excepting that the pins where the heading joins the ground are worked differently. (There is not a continuous working pair, apart from the top section where the new pairs are brought in.) The ground stitch is Torchon with two twists. Diagram 16.5 shows the start of the bookmark.

The bookmark is started this way (following diagram 16.5).

(a) Hang two pairs, one inside the other, around pin 1 and twist each pair twice; these will be the workers for the top border of the bookmark. Hang two pairs around a temporary pin set just below pin 1, and give only one of these pairs a twist; these will be the twisted edge passives for the border. Now hang four pairs on another temporary pin, half way between the previous one and pin 4; these are the untwisted border passives.

(b) Work the pairs on 1 towards the centre (the sequence for each will be cloth-and-twist, cloth stitch, cloth stitch) then work them both together with a cloth stitch, pull-

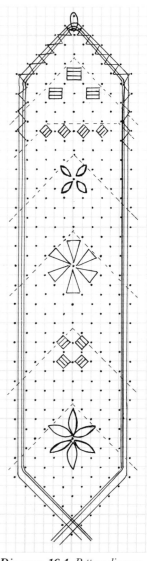

Diagram 16.4 *Pattern diagram for the Tallies and Leaves Bookmark*

Plate 16.2 *The Tallies and Leaves Bookmark*

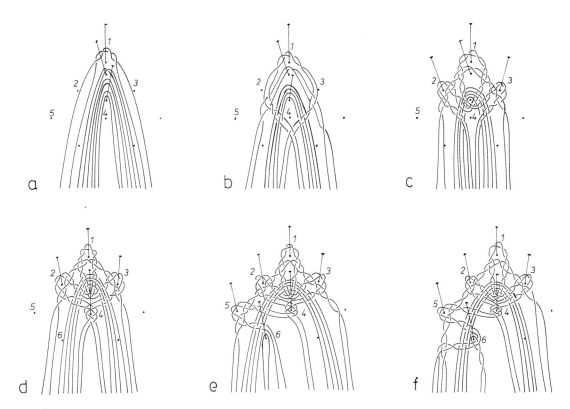

Diagram 16.5 *The various stages in starting the bookmark*

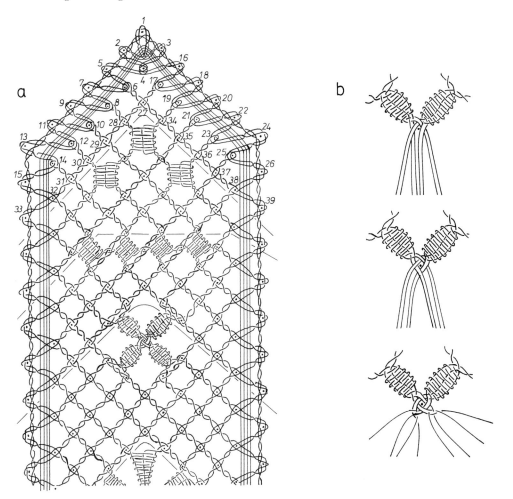

Diagram 16.6 *(a) The working diagram for the top half of the Tallies and Leaves Bookmark;(b) Making a four-pair crossing*

ing the stitch up tight against the temporary pin above.

(c, d) Now work each of these pairs in turn out to the edge pins 2 and 3 (with the reverse of the sequence of stitches in b) and back again, then work them together at 4 with a cloth-and-twist, pin, cloth stitch.

(e, f) After pin 4 leave the right hand pair where it is for the moment and work the left hand pair out to the edge, around pin 5 and back again, passing it to the right of pin 6 around which a new pair should be hung, to be worked in with a single cloth stitch which will turn the border working pair back towards the edge again. All the new pairs are brought in in this way, one pair at each of pins 6, 8, 10, 12, 14 and 17, 19, 21, 23, 25.

After pin 6 continue the bookmark by following work-

ing diagram 16.6 above, paying particular attention to the stitches around the inner headside pins. After pin 39 you will be able to make the first group of tallies, beginning with the top one which uses the pairs from 28 and 34. Because of the size of these tallies and the space they occupy, the pairs entering and leaving them need two twists instead of one. After pin 39 you must plan your own order of working, but there are dotted lines on the pattern diagram to indicate which pins you should work before beginning the next tallies or leaves. The working diagrams should give you most of the information you need to complete the bookmark, but there are a few points you should particularly watch.

For example, where you find tallies or leaves placed at

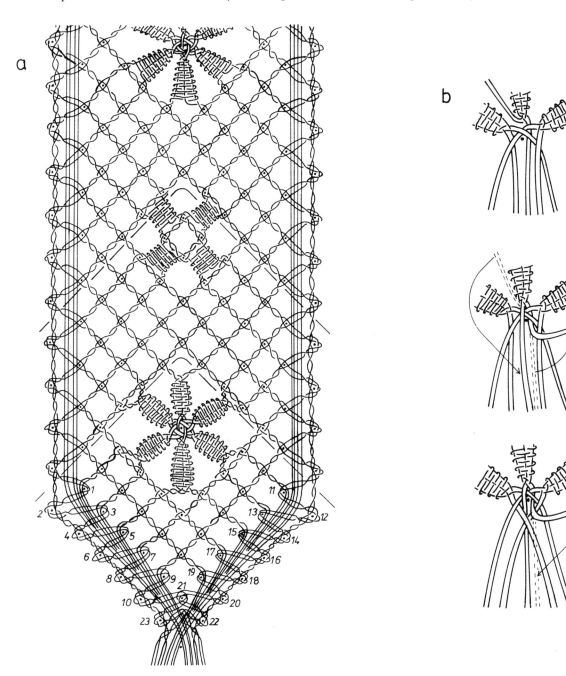

Diagram 16.7 (a) The working diagram for the second half of the Tallies and Leaves Bookmark; (b) Making a six-pair crossing

an angle, rather than parallel with the edge of the pricking, you will need to turn your pillow to work them comfortably, and possibly also push some of the surrounding pins right into the pillow so that they are not in the way. If you then find that you are working over the top of other bobbins, use your working cloth to separate the two layers, or push the bottom layer out of the way.

Also worthy of note are the centres of the flowers. The centre of the first flower has what is known as a four-pair crossing, and the other two have six-pair crossings. In both kinds of crossing each pair of threads is used as a single thread. The four-pair crossing is then a cloth stitch pinned at its centre. In the six-pair crossing a cloth stitch is made with the pairs of the outer two leaves, the pairs of the centre leaf being woven over and under this stitch as it is being made. Diagrams 16.6 and 16.7 show these procedures in detail.

Finally, note that in Sections 4 and 5 the tallies are arranged in such a way that some of them must finish on the right, if you are to avoid involving a weaver thread in the stitches immediately following. I referred to this situation in Section 3 of the Tallies and Leaves Sampler (page 76), and if you look carefully at the working diagram for the bookmark, as well as thinking ahead as you come to the end of each tally, it will become obvious how each must finish.

The bookmark is finished with a point and a single plait made with the eight pairs not disposed of along the bottom borders. Use each two pairs as a single thread and tie off the plait with a collecting knot. The pairs taken out could have been knotted off at the inside border pins 1 to 9 and 11 to 19, to correspond with the pins at which they entered the work inside the top borders, but there is a neater method which is more generally used. If you look carefully at the accompanying diagram you will see that each pair to be disposed of is carried along in the border for a short distance to secure it, and is then cut off. The pair to be removed is always the middle passive pair (of five) and is cut off, or thrown back to be cut off later, after working the rows from the inner edge of the border to the outer edge, beginning with the rows from pin 3 to pin 4 on the left hand side, and pin 13 to 14 on the right hand side.

Fan and Tallies Edging

This edging takes sixteen pairs of bobbins, and may be interpreted in several ways. The tallies are worked in the same way as those at the top of the bookmark. There is no working diagram, but you should not have too much trouble starting if you apply what you have learned in previous exercises.

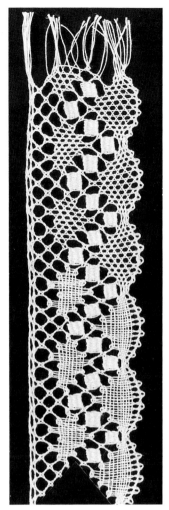

Plate 16.3 *The Fan and Tallies Edging*

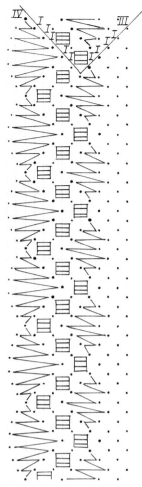

Diagram 16.8 *Pattern diagram for the Fan and Tallies Edging*

17 Trails

Materials:
50/2 or 60/2 linen, or no. 12 Madeira Tanne or equivalent
2.5 mm (10 to the inch) graph paper

First, a word about trails generally. A trail in Torchon lace is usually taken to be a continuous zigzag band of cloth or half stitch, although sometimes other stitches may be used. There are several ways of using trails in a design. Often there will be a single trail dividing one pattern area from another, or a pair of trails one on either side of a pattern area. Sometimes also there may be two trails, each in a different stitch, which may give the appearance of being interwoven around diamonds of some other stitch or motif. Yet another variation is a single trail which divides to pass around a diamond shaped motif of some kind. The following patterns illustrate each of these uses, and you will encounter more when you start looking at other books. The patterns have no working diagrams but each is clearly marked with a starting line. In each pattern starting pins which are not part of the design are marked with a circle, as has been the case in the rest of the book.

The pattern construction is not described in detail in this chapter (or subsequent chapters), so study the pattern diagrams carefully and always begin by marking in the main design elements, then build the rest of the pattern around them. The Roman numerals across the top of the pattern diagrams indicate the number of pairs to be started at each point.

Single Trails

Cloth or half stitch trail

This single trail pattern (diagam 17.1) may be interpreted in several ways, but only two are shown. It is started straight, and the small circles at the top of the pattern diagram indicate support pins for the trail passives. Note that the trail workers start on the left and the diamond worker pair moves to the left after the top pin. The holes in the cloth stitch are worked as for the diamonds of the First Spider and Diamond Insertion (page 48).

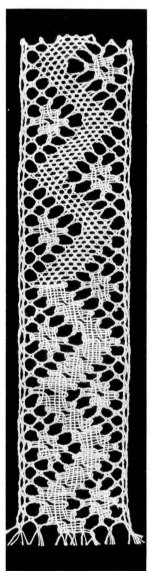

Plate 17.1 *An insertion featuring a single cloth or half stitch trail with small diamonds on either side*

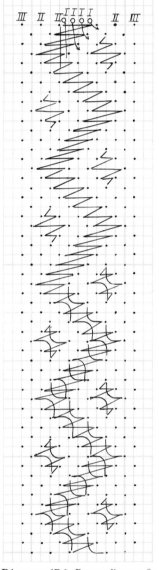

Diagram 17.1 *Pattern diagram for the Single Trail Insertion*

Rose ground trail (diagram 17.2)

Note that along the section of Torchon edge next to the half stitch triangles the triangle working pair is one of the three edge pairs used to work the edge stitches; it then returns to the triangle until needed for the next edge pin.

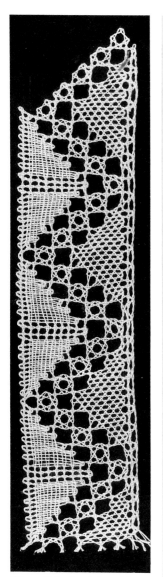

Plate 17.2 *An edging with a rose ground trail and triangles of cloth or half stitch*

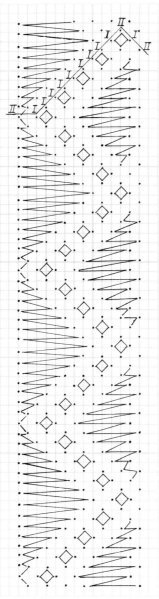

Diagram 17.2 *Pattern diagram for the Rose ground Trail Edging*

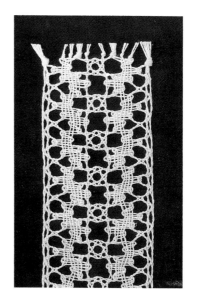

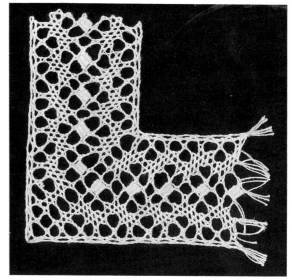

Plate 17.3 *An insertion featuring double (opposing) trails; two different interpretations are shown; one has cloth stitch trails with rose ground, and the other has half stitch trails with tallies between*

Double Trails

The following pattern has two interpretations, and one includes a corner. If you wish to make a complete square it would be better to start along the corner line (diagram 17.3).

It is interesting to note that if all the pattern markings are removed from this design what remains is the basic Torchon mesh grid. A surprising number of different designs is possible using this same basic pattern of pin holes. Why not try it and see?

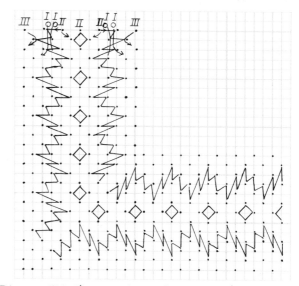

Diagram 17.3 *The pattern diagram for the Double Trails Insertion*

Entwined Trails

Plate 17.4 *An insertion featuring entwined trails, worked in different stitches around a four pair spider*

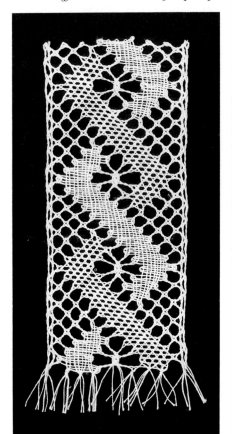

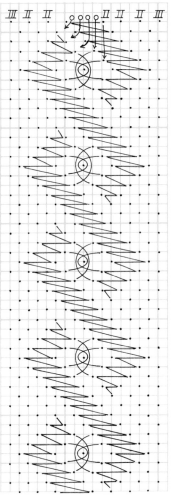

Diagram 17.4 *(left) The pattern diagram for the Entwined Trails Insertion in Plate 17.4*

Plate 17.5 *An edging with a divided trail and stars*

A Divided Trail

This edging has fish-tail fans and a cloth stitch trail which divides around a four-pin diamond containing a star motif, not previously encountered (plate 17.5). The same design, interpreted differently, is used in the chapter on using polar graph paper (Chapter 20).

The worker pair will be travelling from left to right along the row in which the trail divides, and the fifth passive pair will become the trail worker for the right hand side of the trail (plate 17.5 and diagram 17.5a). The dividing pin is worked cloth stitch, pin, cloth stitch.

The star is worked with four pairs, in the following way (diagram 17.5b).

1. Twist all pairs twice.
2. Make the cross movement with the left two pairs.
3. Make the cross movement with the right two pairs.
4. Cloth stitch the right hand pairs through the left hand pairs as for the first half of a spider, but do not pin.
5. Half stitch, and twist the left hand two pairs.
6. Half stitch, and twist the right hand two pairs.

The pairs leave, and return to, the trail as they would for a spider or any other motif.

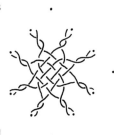

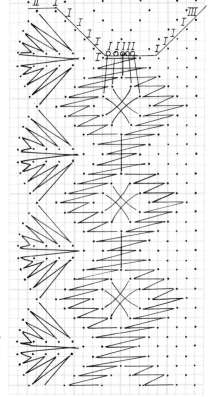

Diagram 17.5
(a) Working diagram for the star motif; (b) Pattern diagram for the Divided Trail Edging

18   Simple Torchon Design

Any Torchon lace pattern may be thought of as a width of basic mesh interrupted by various design elements. The design process actually involves replacing an area of mesh with a particular design element or motif. Generally speaking the design elements of traditional Torchon follow the diagonal lines of the mesh, which limits the shapes available to diamonds and rectangles and their derivatives. (We will leave aside edge treatments for the moment.) These may be thought of as the lace designer's building blocks; they each come in different sizes and may be 'coloured' with different stitches. You will find this analogy even more apt if you actually cut yourself a set of the basic shapes from graph paper, which may be arranged and re-arranged quickly and easily on a basic grid as you experiment with your design.

The aesthetics of lace design are governed by what stitches one uses within the shapes, and by the way the shapes are arranged. The general principles of good design apply to this as to any other art or craft but if you become too preoccupied by such considerations your design will not be a spontaneous expression of yourself. Your own creative mark is more important in the early stages than a studied embodiment of perfect design. When you have worked a sample piece any design faults will be quite obvious to you, and your next effort will be a little better. The principles of good design will thus become a natural part of the way you work, rather than just something you read in a book.

Having said that, there are actually two special points you could keep in mind to save your creative enthusiasm from taking too many hard knocks. Firstly, make sure you take into account the spaces between the stitches as well as the texture of the stitches themselves when designing. Secondly, try to resist the impulse to incorporate all your favourite stitches in the one design!

Clearly, what I have so far said may be applied to any of the geometric laces which have a mesh background, although it may be more helpful for some than for others. Designing your own laces within the various traditional forms is an extremely important part of contemporary lacemaking, and should precede any attempts at experimenting with the modern 'free' laces. Such experiments, without a very thorough understanding of the design and construction of the more formal laces, are bound to be frustrating.

The Building Blocks of Simple Torchon Design

Gimp Threads

These may be used alone as the only design element, or as an outline to other design elements.

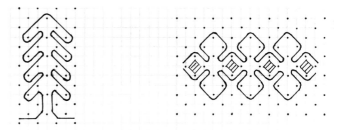

Diagram 18.1 *Using a gimp as the main design element*

Diamond Shapes

Diamond shapes are the most fundamental design elements. The size of a diamond is usually described by the number of pin holes along each of its sides.

Two-pin diamonds

These are obviously the smallest diamonds possible; they can be worked as tallies (in either direction), or as tiny cloth or half stitch 'spots' (workers moving to right or left

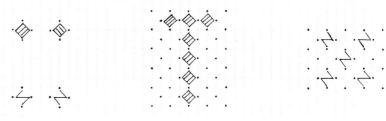

Diagram 18.2 *Two-pin diamonds, alone and grouped*

after the top pin). They may be used singly, perhaps to relieve a large area of plain ground, or grouped into other shapes.

Three-pin diamonds

These can be worked as honeycomb (which you have not previously encountered), a large tally, a single leaf, or a cloth or half stitch diamond. They can also be grouped into larger shapes. (Single honeycombs or honeycomb groups must be spaced off cloth or half stitch or they lose their definition.)

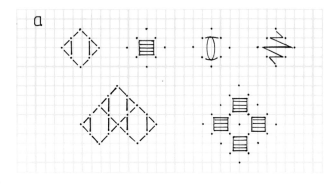

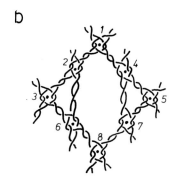

Diagram 18.3 (a) Three-pin diamonds; (b) A single unit of honeycomb

Four-pin diamonds

The possibilities for these are more numerous and include spiders, a single rose ground rose, clover (see chapter 20), a star, cloth or half stitch and small flowers. These can also be grouped, or used with other elements.

Five-pin diamonds

These may be worked as spiders, cloth or half stitch diamonds, six-petal flowers, a group of four honeycombs, a checkerboard grouping of tallies, and so on. In general, the larger the diamond the more desirable it will be to break it up into smaller shapes, or to choose more complicated stitches.

Rectangles

Rectangles are always placed diagonally in Torchon lace, and can be almost any size. They can also be worked in any stitch, and may be placed together to form a trail, a chevron shape, or a diamond shaped border for other stitches. (If you use cut-out shapes to plan your design the rectangles may be butt-joined or overlapped to plan trails and their variants.)

Triangles

A triangle is best thought of as a diamond cut in half vertically. If you use a triangle on the headside (or footside) edge of a design the number of edge pins will be the same as for a fan of otherwise similar dimensions (diagram 18.7a). Triangles within the design cannot have a really sharp vertical edge unless you add an extra pin hole at the apex. This can look clumsy. Diagram 18.7b shows the more usual way of working a triangle within the ground.

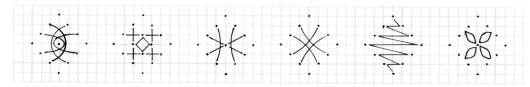

Diagram 18.4 Four-pin diamonds

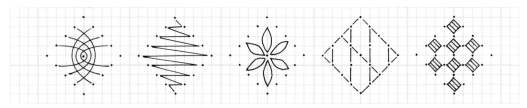

Diagram 18.5 Five-pin diamonds

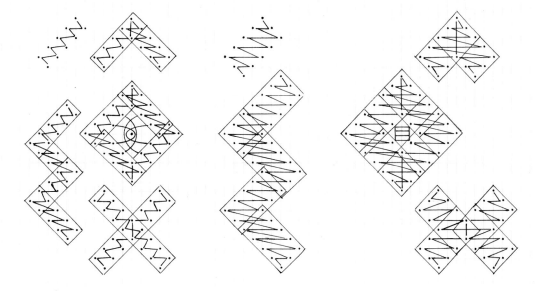

Diagram 18.6 *Rectangle shapes combined in different ways*

Edge Treatments

Apart from straight headings the most common edge treatments are simple fans, fishtail fans, scallops and points, although you will encounter others. There is a fundamental difference in the effect of fans and scallops or points; fans tend to dominate a design visually, whereas scallops or points minimise the visual impact of the edge so that the ground and other elements become the most important features of the design. Within reason, fans and scallops may be any size.

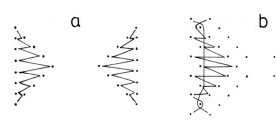

Diagram 18.7 *Triangle shapes*

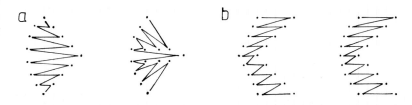

Diagram 18.8 *(a) Fans and (b) points and scallops*

Other Shapes

Most Torchon designs work within the basic diagonal lines of the mesh, but it is quite possible to depart from this with circles, and even squares. It is also very rewarding to experiment with stitches not normally associated with Torchon, such as the old Binche spiders and Toile stars illustrated in *Bobbin Lace Stitches*, page 212 onwards. (See the Reading List on page 104.)

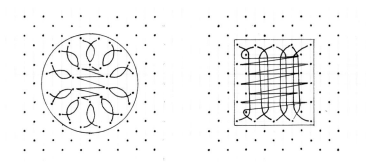

Diagram 18.9 *A circle and a square*

19 Beginnings and Endings

If you have worked through all the exercises in the book so far you will have encountered most of the possible ways of starting and finishing a piece of lace. This chapter summarises those methods and introduces some extra decorative ones which you may find useful for particular purposes.

Nominating a Starting Line

Each of the exercises in the book includes an explanation of where and how to start working, and in most instances the actual starting line is marked on the pattern diagram. If you have designed a pattern of your own, or acquired an unmarked pattern from another source, you must make such decisions for yourself.

There is always more than one way to start any piece of lace, and whichever you choose must take into account the design of the lace as well as its intended use. In many cases it will be appropriate to start in a straight line across the pattern, especially if the ends of the lace are to be enclosed in a straight seam. However, if the finishing threads are to be tied off into the starting loops, as is the case for a square or circular piece, then a straight start is not advis-

able as it makes the join too obvious. A straight start can be unwise for other reasons too; for example, if it involves starting in the middle of a spider.

Instead, consider starting diagonally, or in a broken diagonal line along the edge of a pattern repeat. The advantage of the latter over a full diagonal start is that it is not spread out over so much of the pattern. Diagram 19.1 shows several possible starts for the one design. In each case the line is drawn just above the starting pin holes, as has been the custom throughout the book.

Most patterns can be started diagonally, except for the start of a continuous or divided trail, or edge scallop. These must be started horizontally, although other areas of the design may be started diagonally. The Rose Ground and Scallops Edging in Chapter 15 and the Divided Trail Edging in Chapter 17 are examples of such a start.

Calculating the Number of Pairs

The basis for working out how many pairs you will need is, firstly, that in standard Torchon laces the number of pairs used is constant throughout, and secondly, that two pairs work the stitches at each pin of the basic Torchon

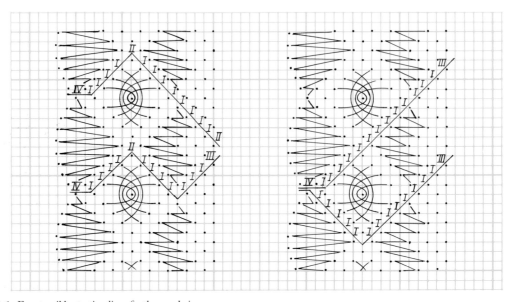

Diagram 19.1 *Four possible starting lines for the one design*

mesh grid. Areas of the mesh may have been replaced with something else during the design process, which means that some of the pin holes are omitted (for example within a cloth stitch diamond) but this does not usually alter the number of pairs needed.

When one encounters an unmarked pattern, calculating how many pairs it takes is part of working out the whole starting procedure. For that reason the diagram for the section on starting lines also indicates how many pairs start at each pin. You will notice that where two diagonals converge upwards two pairs must start, and one pair starts at each pin along the diagonals; where diagonals converge downwards no pairs start, as the stitch at that point is worked with pairs which have already entered the work. It should be easy to extrapolate from this and other exercises in the book for almost any Torchon pattern you may encounter, but should you wish to work out how many pairs you will need without all the other starting details the following method is very useful.

If your pattern has been drawn on graph paper, rule a vertical line through the footside pin holes for a short distance. Then rule another vertical line opposite it along the headside edge (or the other footside in the case of an insertion). On a pattern for an edging with a straight heading the line will pass through all the headside pin holes; on a simple fan or scalloped edge pattern the line will pass along the outer edge of the curves; on a fish-tail fan pattern rule the line through the pin holes between the fans (remember, the latter does not use extra pairs to fill the curve).

Next mark in the counting line horizontally between the other two, beginning at a pin hole (or pin hole position) on the headside line. Finally, starting at the headside edge count two pairs for each pin hole, or pin hole position, along the counting line; or as one of my friends says 'count two pairs for every pin hole whether it's there or not!' Allow one extra pair if the footside edge is beyond the last pin hole on the line because it is half way to what would be the next pin hole along the line if the lace were wider.

Having thus established the basic number of pairs for the given pattern width it only remains to decide whether you must add extra pairs for either footside or headside edge treatments; for example, one extra pair would be needed as passives for a standard Torchon edge, and one or two extra pairs as passives for a straight heading. Diagram 19.2 shows how the pairs are counted on several different patterns.

If your pattern is not drawn on graph paper it is still possible to use the same method, especially if there is an uninterrupted line of pin holes across the pattern; even if there is not, it is usually possible to estimate the pin hole positions. It is also possible to use the method in reverse when designing. For example, if you have only nineteen pairs of bobbins spare and you reserve one as the passive pair for the Torchon edge, then you know that your pattern must finish 18 divided by $2 = 9$ pin holes wide, and you can design accordingly.

Starting with Knots

Despite what you may read to the contrary elsewhere, starting a straight piece of lace with the pairs knotted together is a practical and time saving alternative to re-coupling bobbins cut from previous work. The re-coupling involves knotting the bobbins together in pairs, and winding the knot onto one bobbin or the other, then dealing with it in the prescribed manner as it emerges in the lace. Quite apart from the time it takes to re-couple the bobbins it seems to me to be more desirable to avoid joins in the lace than to avoid starting with knots.

The simplest knotted start involves tying together all the pairs needed at any one pin with a single knot, and pinning through the knot so that it will not slide around as you work. The knot then takes the place of the stitch or stitches ordinarily worked around the starting pins. Another equally satisfactory method is to knot the threads together in fours (two pairs) around pins set in the pillow a

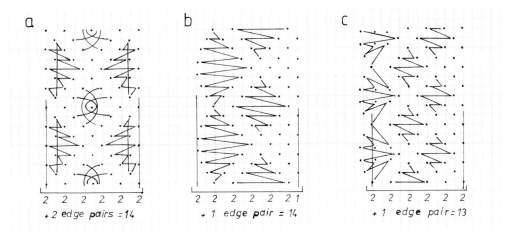

Diagram 19.2 *Counting the number of pairs needed to work different patterns: (a) An insertion; (b) A simple fan edging; (c) A fish-tail fan edging*

short distance above the pattern, and plait down to the starting pins which are then enclosed by the appropriate stitches.

Starting with the Bobbins Coupled

Obviously if you are winding your bobbins from scratch for a new piece of lace it is sensible to couple them, and absolutely essential to do so if the lace is to be joined up at the end, since it halves the number of knots you would otherwise have. If you still have plenty of suitable thread on your bobbins from a previous project re-couple them as previously described, or make a new pair from each wound bobbin by winding half its thread on to an empty bobbin.

There are examples in the book of a wide variety of coupled starts to which you should refer when deciding how best to start a new pattern; you are bound to find the information you need, although you may have to combine techniques from more than one exercise. As a general rule the starting stitches must be consistent with what is to follow, and the bobbins must be arranged on the pricking to enable this to happen. For example, you may need to hang the pairs temporarily on pins set in any convenient pin hole above the starting line, so that you can then make exactly the same stitches around the starting pins as you would if you were proceeding from completed work. If you are starting at the very top of the pricking you may add extra holes for support pins, in which case the holes should be circled to indicate that they are not part of the pattern. You will also need to do this to start passive pairs across an area of cloth or half stitch. Usually the support pins are removed once the starting stitches have been made, enabling the starting loops to be pulled down around the starting pins, but extra pins which support passives across cloth or half stitch are usually best left in place, especially in the case of a square or circular edging or mat where all the starting loops must be clearly visible for the tying-off process.

Finishing

The simplest way to finish a straight length of lace is to knot the ends together, either with a collecting knot or an overhand knot, as was suggested for most of the samples in the book. Another simple finish is to plait the pairs before knotting, as shown for the Spiders Bookmark (page 46).

A square or circular piece is also finished with knots, the ends being very carefully threaded through the starting loops before tying off. The notes and diagrams for the Square Edging describe this tying-off process in detail (page 59), and although other laces may be different the same principles apply, which may be summarised as follows: tie off each ground stitch or footside edge pair into the middle of the appropriate starting stitch, and tie off passive and worker pairs singly into their starting loops. Without exception the same number of pairs ties off at a given point as started at that point, and the only sign of the join in your lace should be the actual knot; in every other respect the working must be continuous. Achieving this is easier said than done and requires the utmost care and attention, not just at the join but before you even start the lace.

Two methods of disposing of the thread ends were described at the end of the Square Edging exercise, namely, darning the ends in or cutting them off close to the knot. These methods have been used by generations of lacemakers, but in my opinion neither is ideal for heavy thread laces; the former looks too clumsy and the latter is not really secure enough for articles which will be laundered frequently. An alternative method which is becoming increasingly popular with modern lacemakers works as follows. After tying off in the normal manner cut off the bobbins, leaving several centimetres (2"–3") of thread beyond each knot. Then take a needle and fine thread the same colour as the lace and, working from headside to footside on the wrong side, oversew the ends neatly and tightly along the joining line, binding in each pair for only half a centimetre (¹/₄") before laying it aside to be cut off, so that no more than two pairs are carried along at a time. This method works best if the join is along a row of ground stitches, but with care it can also accommodate the ends at the edge of, or across, cloth and half stitch less conspicuously than when they are darned in. Plate 11.4 on page 59 shows the discarded threads before they are cut off, to give you an idea of how the number of bound pairs stays constant along the join.

Starting and Finishing with a Hem

The sample in Plate 19.1 and its accompanying pattern diagram 19.3 show a simple way to start and finish a length of lace with a hem, which will neatly hide all knots and

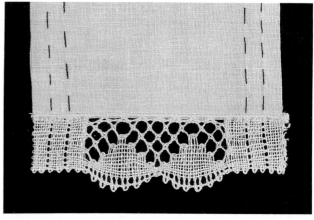

Plate 19.1 *Starting and finishing a piece of lace with a hem*

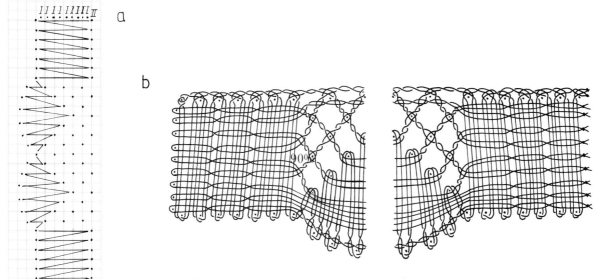

Diagram 19.3 *(a) Hem sections added to a simple fan pattern. The pattern may be extended by adding more fans; (b) Working diagram for the hem section*

loose ends. In fact the lace may be started as well as finished with knots, if that is more convenient.

Each hem section consists of a block of thirteen rows of cloth stitch (with a straight footside) divided into three by twists on the passive pairs between rows 4 and 5, and 8 and 9. The twists mark the fold lines of the hem and should line up with the fold lines of the fabric the lace is to be sewn to. The sample in the photograph is mounted ready for both fabric and lace to be hemmed in the one operation as would be appropriate for a tray cloth or table mat. With a little thought this method may be adapted for any piece of lace, and the hem width may be varied by working more or less rows of cloth stitch between the twists.

The sample in the photograph has been machine-stitched to the fabric with a very narrow satin stitch (one-quarter the normal width) over the footside edge pair only. The excess fabric was then cut away close to the lace on the wrong side. (This method works just as well if the satin stitching is done by hand.) The black basting stitches indicate the fold lines for the fabric hem, and line up with the fold lines in the lace.

Starting the Torchon Edge from a Point

Strictly speaking it is not possible to work a Torchon edge along a diagonal, but the sample in plate 19.2 and diagrams 19.4, 19.5 and 19.6 demonstrate a near approximation of it for use when a shaped insertion is required. It has a straight edge which can be easily sewn to the fabric. Such a technique is useful for working insertions for a dress or blouse where the finishing threads of the lace can be enclosed in a hem or seam. The sample uses ten pairs of bobbins which must be coupled.

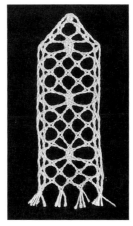

Plate 19.2 *The shaped insertion sample, in which the Torchon edge is started from a point*

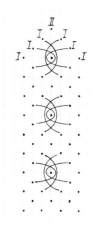

Diagram 19.4 *The pattern diagram for the shaped insertion sample*

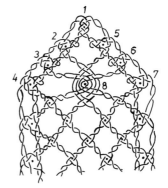

Diagram 19.5 *General working diagram for the shaped insertion sample*

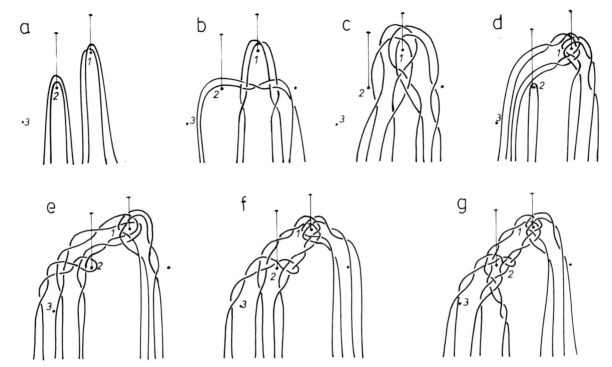

Diagram 19.6 *The starting procedure for the shaped insertion sample*

The pairs are started as follows:

(a) Hang two pairs on pin 1 and twist one of them once. Hang two more pairs temporarily on pin 2.

(b) Work the right hand pair on pin 2 through both pairs on pin 1 in cloth-and-twist.

(c) Now pass the remaining pair on pin 2 behind pin 1 and lay it down to the right of the other three. Check that the two outermost pairs each have two twists, and the others have one twist. The two pairs now on the right are laid aside to work down the right hand diagonal, and the two on the left work down the left diagonal.

(d) Pass these left hand pairs to the left of pin 2, upon which should be hung one new pair.

(e) Work the new pair to the left through the other two pairs in cloth-and-twist.

(f) Take out pin 2, but replace it between the inner two pairs as shown.

(g) Now enclose the pin with these two pairs. Check that each of the pairs is twisted as shown. The innermost pair is laid aside to work into the lace later, and the other two continue along to pin 3 where another new pair must be brought in exactly as for pin 2. After pin 4, the new pairs are brought in along the right hand diagonal, using the mirror image of the procedure for the left hand side. After pins 4 and 7, the edge pins are worked as for the standard Torchon edge.

Starting and Finishing 'Invisibly' along the Torchon Edge

The sample in plate 19.3 is a rectangular piece of lace with three headside edges and one footside edge. It is adapted from an edging pattern by the addition of a corner turn at each end, which is terminated in line with the original footside. The work starts and finishes at opposite ends of the footside, enabling the finishing threads to be disposed of securely and invisibly when the lace is mounted, whatever the mounting method used.

Lace constructed in this way might be used to trim a table mat, tray cloth or hand towel, or as a decoration for a pocket flap or cuff on a dress or blouse. It may also be used for collars, in which case the chosen Torchon pattern must be plotted on polar graph paper. When the collar is completed, the finishing ends are enclosed in the bias neckband by which it is attached to the neck facing of the garment.

Hiding the ends of straight items will depend on the mounting method you choose. For example, where the fabric-hemming and lace-mounting are to be completed in the one operation the ends are trimmed to 1 cm (³/₈″), and simply caught in with the stitching, but when the fabric is hemmed first and the lace then slip-stitched to the outer fold of the hem, the ends are afterwards threaded inside the hem with a needle.

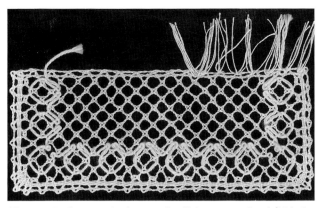

Plate 19.3 *A rectangular lace sample which was started and finished along the Torchon edge*

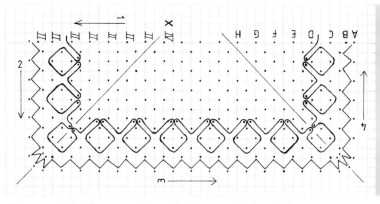

Diagram 19.7 *The pattern diagram for the rectangular lace in plate 19.3. The pattern may be extended by adding to the section between the corner lines*

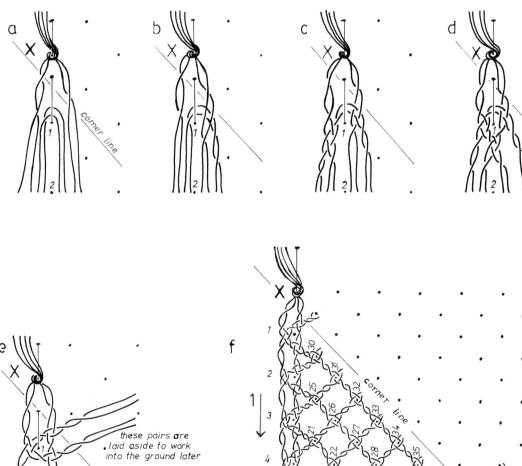

these pairs are laid aside to work into the ground later

these pairs are now ready to work pin 2

Diagram 19.8 *Starting pairs along the Torchon edge*

Make the pattern and pricking as usual (diagram 19.7), and pin the pricking to the centre of your pillow, with arrow 1 pointing towards you. Wind eighteen pairs of bobbins, coupled, with the usual thread, and one gimp bobbin, and begin working as follows (diagram 19.8):

(a) Hang four pairs around temporary pin X and divide them by passing one bobbin of each pair (four bobbins) to the back of the pillow, making a couple of turns around the pin as you go to secure the threads. The right hand pair of the four threads now hanging

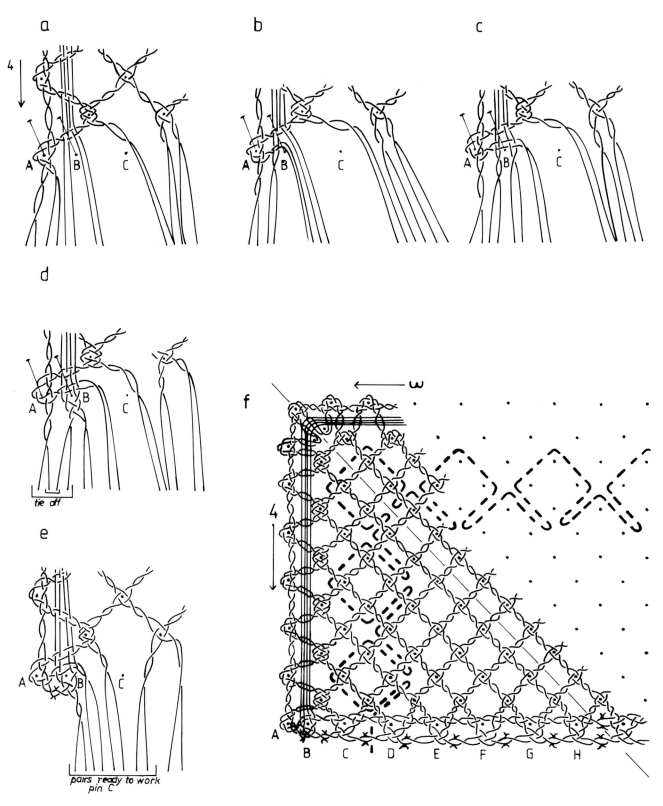

Diagram 19.9 *Finishing pairs along the Torchon edge*

in front of the pin becomes the edge passive pair, the left hand pair will be the alternating edge pair. (The pairs behind the pin will be the continuation of these, later, for the section of footside between the corner lines.) Hang two more pairs on pin 1 and twist one of them once. There are now four pairs hanging before you. Next, making each stitch a cloth-and-twist, work together *(b)* the right hand two pairs, *(c)* the left hand two pairs, and *(d)* the middle two pairs.

(e) The two pairs on the right after these stitches are laid aside to work into the ground later, and the remaining two pairs continue on to work with two new pairs hung on pin 2, exactly as for pin 1.

(f) Continue in this way until all the pairs have been brought in, remembering to work in the gimp between pins 5 and 6.

After the last pairs have been added at pin 7, work cloth-and-twist above and below pin 8, then turn both pillow and diagram so that arrow 2 is facing you, and work the section up to the corner line. Turn pillow and diagram again and work to the next corner line, making quite sure that you unwind the pairs round pin X and adjust their twists before working them in. Note that the gimp works into the lace in much the same way as for the small square mat in Chapter 15. Full representation of this is omitted here to avoid confusion in the diagram.

Continue the sample, turning the second corner in mirror image of the first, until you have worked all excepting pins B to H, then finish as follows (diagram 19.9):

(a) Isolate as far as possible the four left hand pairs, arranging them in the order shown. Push all remaining pins into the pillow to make the working easier.

(b) Then, making each stitch a cloth-and-twist, work together the middle two pairs (and pin between),

(c) the right hand two pairs, and finally,

(d) the middle two pairs.

(e) The left hand two pairs are now tied off (in such a way that their twists are preserved) and the next two ground stitch pairs are separated out to be worked with the continuing pairs at pin C.

(f) After pin H, when all the ground stitch pairs have been disposed of in this way, two pairs of passive threads will remain to be tied off together, as well as two edge pairs.

A straight heading pattern was chosen as the simplest to adapt to this method. If you wish to adapt a pattern with scallops or fans on the headside a little bit of fiddling may be necessary to start and finish the headside passives satisfactorily.

20 Using Polar Graph Paper

Polar graph paper is a series of concentric circles drawn at fixed intervals (usually 1 or 2 mm) and intersected by radial lines at one degree intervals. The distance between these radial lines increases with their distance from the centre of the circles, and the distortion thus produced means that all the diagonals will be curved rather than straight. In lace this gives a delightful effect, but within a particular piece it may also mean that the thread appropriate for the size of the grid along the inner edge of the curve may be too thin for the expanded grid along the outer curve.

Apart from designing only narrow circular pieces, there are several simple ways of overcoming this. One is to choose the thread suitable for the grid in the middle of the pattern, so that the distortion is spread in two directions. Another is to choose stitches which will stand a little distortion, or use design elements which will allow the addition of extra pairs, or heavier thread, in the sparser part of the lace.

The Circular Edging

Materials:
50/2 or 60/2 linen, or no. 12 Madeira Tanne or equivalent
2.5 mm (10 to the inch) *polar* graph paper

Bobbins:
22 pairs

The working of the Circular Edging in plate 20.1 illustrates the corrective measures outlined above. It is, in fact, a different interpretation of the pattern for the Divided Trail Edging in Chapter 17 (page 81). The trail is worked in half stitch, which distorts in a pleasing way, and two extra pairs were added to the trail to give it more weight. (These must be taken into account when dividing the trail.) The dividing pin is worked half stitch, pin, half stitch. Fishtail fans cope with the circular distortion better than other fans, and are worked normally in this sample, but it would have been possible to use a slightly heavier thread for the fan workers to give a more robust-looking edge to the lace.

The sample uses a different motif in each diamond to illustrate a range of possibilities; it is probably not a good idea to use them all in the one finished piece of lace. The scale of the sample is the same as for the straight version, as far as they can be compared. It will make a circular edging for a mat which will finish about 20 cm (8") in diameter.

The basis for deciding on the size of thread is similar to that for straight lace, except that the only fixed dimension of the grid is the equivalent of the horizontal one on a straight lace, that is, the distance between the pin holes of the grid along one of the radial lines. On this pattern these are 5 mm ($^1/_5$") apart (2 graph paper spaces). See diagram 20.1.

Many of the patterns in the rest of the book could be drafted on polar graph paper, providing the number of pin holes in each repeat of the design is divisible into 360. Some would look more attractive than others, depending on the stitches used. For example, rose ground used as a ground stitch does not adapt well to the circular format, nor do simple cloth stitch fans, unless they are very small.

The clover filling is worked with four pairs of threads, thus:
1. Twist each pair twice.
2. Work cloth-and-twist with the left two pairs.
3. Work cloth-and-twist with the right two pairs.
4. Work half stitch, pin, half stitch with the middle two pairs.
5. Work cloth stitch and two twists with the left two pairs.
6. Work cloth stitch and two twists with the right two pairs.

Collars and Polar Graph Paper

Any Torchon edging pattern for which a suitable corner can be designed may be drafted on polar graph to make a collar pattern. The collar may then be started and finished along the footside (neck) edge as described in Chapter 19.

The neck edge of the average adult collar, for a garment with a high neckline, is plotted on a radius of between 8 and 9 cm (3"–3$^1/_2$"), and generally extends through 300° of the circle, depending on how the pattern repeats fall. It is only necessary to draft half of a two-piece collar which will extend through about 150°. Two-piece collars often fit better than one-piece collars, and are certainly easier to work on a conventional pillow.

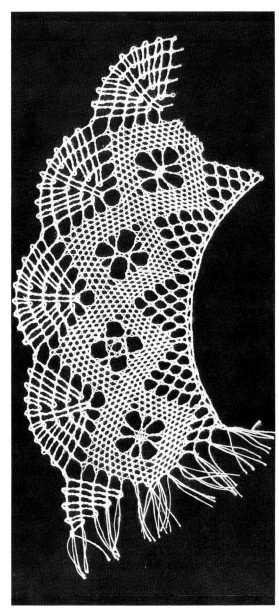

Plate 20.1 *Section of the Circular Edging, based on the Divided Trail Edging in Chapter 17*

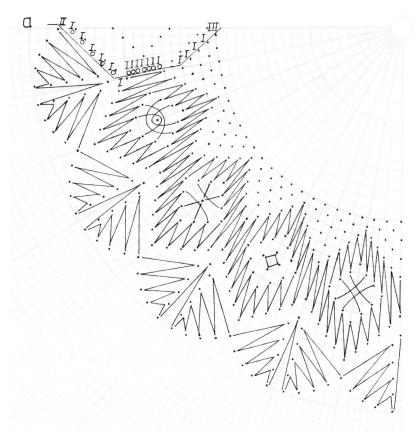

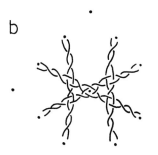

Diagram 20.1 *(a) Pattern diagram for the Circular Edging; (b) Working diagram for the clover filling*

If you do decide on a one-piece collar you will need to divide the pricking into two or three pieces, depending on the size of your pillow, and move the work up when you come to the end of each section.

Some suppliers sell a special pillow for working collars on. It is shaped like a fan and the surface is divided into three equal movable blocks which can be interchanged so that the relative position of the working area remains constant. The tiresome procedure of moving up is therefore avoided.

A collar for a wide neckline needs to be drafted differently to fit properly, and is rather beyond the scope of a beginners' book. It is not simply a matter of using a bigger radius.

Gimp and Tallies Collar

Materials:
30/2 linen or equivalent, and No. 3 cotton perle gimp
  or
35/2 or 40/2 linen or equivalent, and no. 5 cotton perle gimp
2 mm *polar* graph

Bobbins:
18 pairs plus 1 gimp pair

The Gimp and Tallies Collar has a straight heading and the ground stitches are Torchon with two twists. The stitches enclosed by the gimp on either side of the tallies are worked in twisted half stitch ground. See plate 20.2 and diagram 20.2.

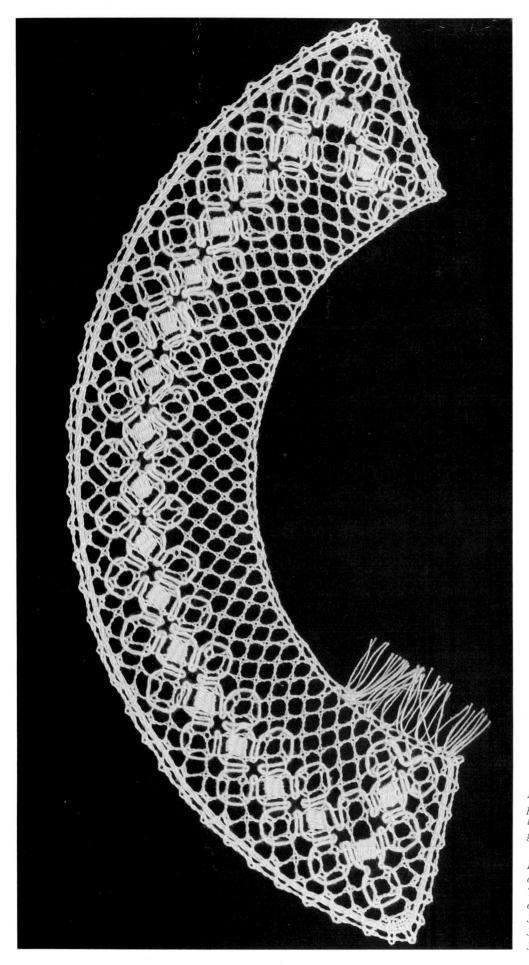

Plate 20.2 *Half of a two-piece collar with gimp and tallies, to fit a size 12 or 14 garment*

Diagram 20.2 *Pattern diagram for the Gimp and Tallies Collar: (a) Drafted over 4 spaces of the graph for 30/2 linen; (b) Drafted over 3 spaces of the graph for 35/2 or 40/2 linen*

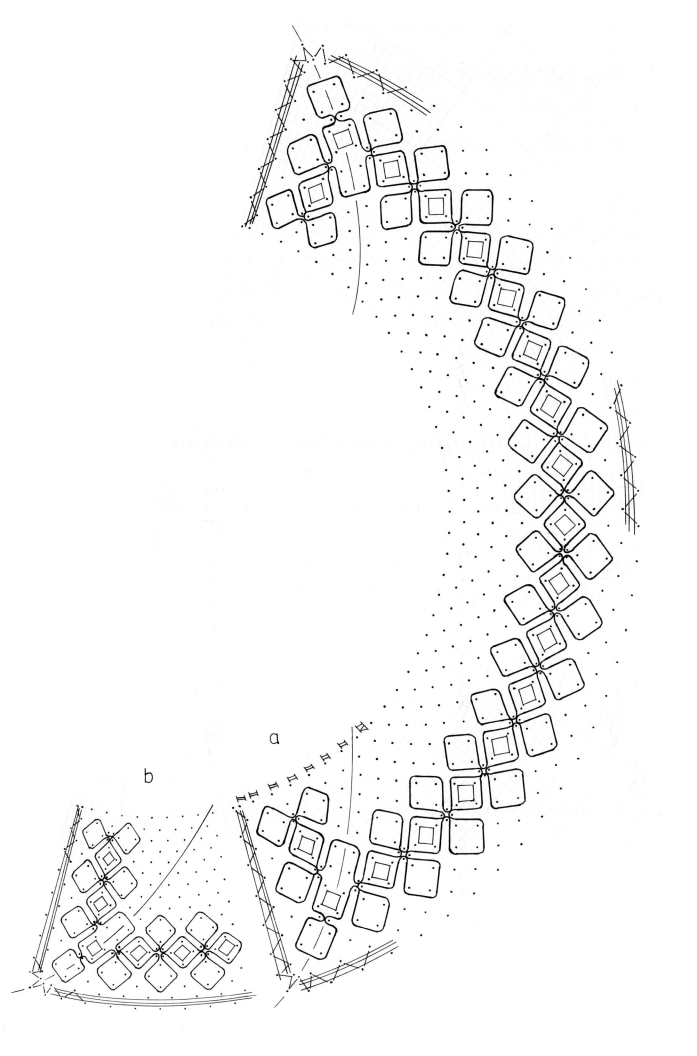

a

b

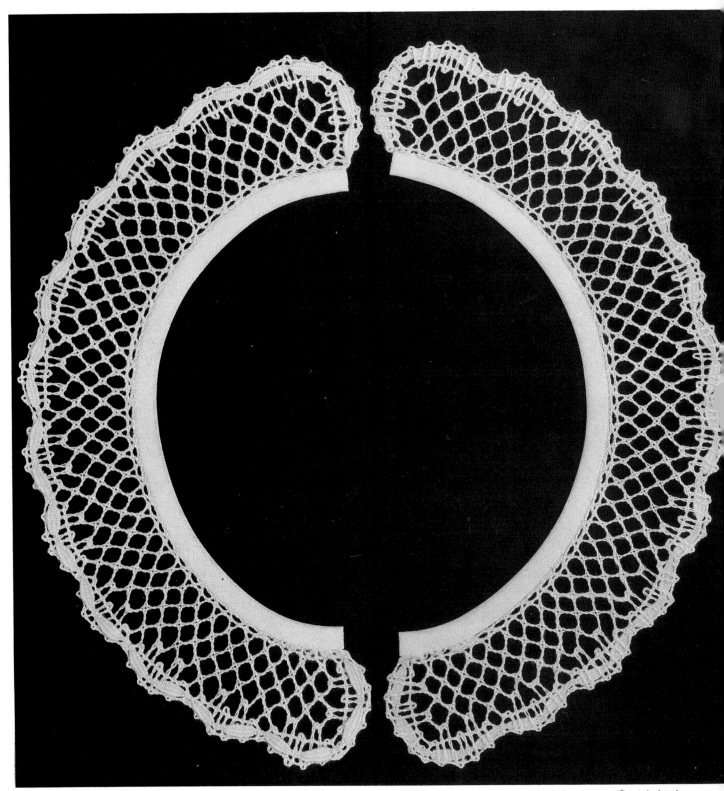

Plate 20.3 *The Child's Collar with neck binding attached. The binding is stitched to the neck facing so that it only the lace is seen. The right hand side of the collar is placed wrong side up to show the arrangement of the leaves. The collar was designed and worked by Brenda Chad*

a

Child's Collar

Materials:
30/2 linen or equivalent, and No. 3 cotton
perle gimp
    or
35/2 or 40/2 linen or equivalent, and no. 5
cotton perle gimp
2 mm *polar* graph

Bobbins:
12 pairs

Again the ground stitches are Torchon with
two twists, and the edge treatment is a kind
of fan, worked in cloth-and-twist, with two
leaves worked in relief over each one. The
leaves are formed with the extra fan passives,
and are only worked into the fan at their points.
The photograph shows clearly both right and
wrong sides of the collar so you can see how
this is done. See plate 20.3 and diagram 20.3.

b

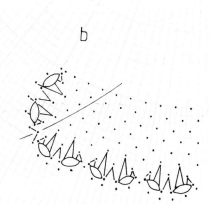

Diagram 20.3 *Pattern diagram for the Child's
Collar: (a) Drafted over 4 graph spaces for 30/2 linen;
(b) Drafted over 3 graph spaces for use with 35/2 or
40/2 linen*

21 Mounting Lace

How to mount one's finished lace could easily be the subject of a book on its own, so only a few simple suggestions are made here. Whatever method you choose, be sure to wash the fabric first to pre-shrink it, and when stitching be careful not to stretch the lace. In fact the lace should be just a fraction longer than the fabric to which it is sewn.

Mounting on the Edge of a Hem-stitched Hem

The photograph of the Square Edging in Chapter 11 (page 56) shows it mounted on a small square of linen which was first hemmed with an ornamental drawn-work hem stitch. Instruction in this kind of hemming will be found in most embroidery books as well as in the inexpensive Coats Anchor booklet '100 Embroidery Stitches' (page 36). The lace is slip-stitched to the outer fold of the hem. This is a modern and effective way to mount straight or square pieces of lace, and is suitable for most kinds of fabric, but especially for open-weave linens.

Satin Stitching or Buttonholing

Plate 19.1 on page 88, illustrating how to begin and end a piece of lace with a hem, shows the lace satin-stitched to the fabric by machine. Many purists will be horrified by this but I am inclined to think we must move with the times. Besides, should you wish to remove the lace for use on another article, the machine satin stitching is much easier to unpick than the hand worked kind, which has always been one of the accepted methods for mounting lace. Satin stitching is suitable for most fabrics, and may be used with equal success on straight and shaped laces. If you prefer it, buttonhole stitch may be used instead, but it takes longer to work, and in my opinion is more obtrusive. Before the final stitching baste the lace firmly in place on the fabric, which should be about 1 cm (³/₈") larger all around than needed, using small stitches taken very close to the footside passive threads. When the satin stitching is completed, cut the excess fabric close to the stitching on the wrong side.

Slip-hemming and Overcasting

This method is my personal favourite because it is strong and unobtrusive, and works on all fabrics, and for straight or shaped laces. It also allows the lace to be removed easily

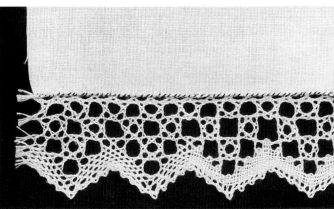

Plate 21.1 *The lace slip-hemmed to the fabric after basting (top) and (bottom) the fabric trimmed and overcast into the back of the slip-hemming*

and safely should the need arise. First cut the fabric 1 cm (³/₈") larger all around than necessary, and baste the lace firmly to it with small stitches, close to the footside. Next slip-hem the lace to the fabric over the footside edge threads. These two processes are shown worked in black thread in the upper photograph in plate 21.1.

Finally, remove the basting thread and cut away all but 2 mm (¹/₁₆") of the excess fabric on the wrong side, then overcast the raw edge, catching only the back of the hemming stitches as you do so. This process is shown in black thread in the lower photograph in plate 21.1.

Appliqué

The Rose ground and Gimp insertion in Chapter 14 (page 68) looks most effective when mounted on top of the fabric rather than set into it. This would probably be the case for most insertions with straight headings in place of the Torchon edge. The mounting is best accomplished by stitching between the untwisted edge passives along both sides of the lace, either by hand or machine.

22   *A Taste of Free Lace*

Materials:
Any of the linen threads you have been using would be suitable for this exercise. No graph paper is needed.

Bobbins:
12 pairs approximately, depending on the thread used.

Before you get too used to working within the discipline of laces which are made over a regular grid it is quite a good idea to have some understanding of working in a free way with just an outline of the shape to guide you; that is, with no graph paper and without a pre-planned pattern of pin holes. To many of you this will seem quite terrifying, but please give it a try. It is not nearly as difficult as you may think. In fact I regularly take my new students through this exercise after the First Braid in Chapter 4.

Working a Leaf Shape

A long thin leaf shape is ideal to start experimenting with. In Australia we are inevitably drawn to gum leaves which can be anything from 8 cm to 28 cm (3"–11") in length. If you do not feel confident of your drawing ability find a leaf and trace around it, marking the leaf rib down the centre. Sandwich the drawing or tracing between card and clear plastic film in the usual way and pin it to your pillow with the tip of the leaf at the top.

For the best effect leaves need to be worked with a footside edge. If you choose to work in colour the three worker pairs should probably be brown or rusty red, and the passives different (closely related) shades of green.

Spacing the pin holes

In working a shape like this you should aim to have the pins along each edge staggered in relation to each other instead of horizontally opposite as they were for the braid exercises. In fact having the pins horizontally opposite each other is only really appropriate in the context of Torchon and other grid-based laces. In free lace (and most braid laces) the pins need to be staggered so that each row of stitches is approximately the same length. In practice this will mean that if your leaf shape is curved the pin holes

will need to be further apart on the outside of the curve and closer together on the inside of the curve.

It really is best to position the pin holes as you go for this kind of lacemaking as this will give you the best understanding of the relationship between thread size and distance between pins, and allows for much more creativity. For example, if the mood takes you to switch from cloth stitch to half stitch you may find the pins need to be closer together. If you have spaced them all equally beforehand you will not be able to do this.

Most new lacemakers tend to crowd their first attempts at free lace by working the pins too close together. You should try to avoid this; remember you are making lace, not weaving! The end result will be much more appealing if the stitches are all clearly distinguishable.

Setting in the workers to start the leaf

Follow diagram 22.1 and work as follows:
(a) Hang 2 pairs on pin A and plait for the tip of the leaf, finishing with each pair twisted. Hang a third pair on pin B between the threads of the left hand pair.
(b) Twist each new pair thus formed once. The three pairs now on the pillow are the workers and will form the footside edge.
(c) Take the middle pair and work it through the right hand plait pair in cloth stitch and leave it twisted. Pin at C to the left of this stitch. The pair next to the pin becomes the worker for the first row.

Adding passives and working the body of the leaf

Hang the first passive pair on D which is on the mid-line of the leaf (diagram 22.1c). More are added as the leaf widens, always along the mid-line, and exactly halfway through the threads (diagram 22.1d). This will sometimes mean separating the threads of an existing pair. Keep adding pairs until the widest part of the leaf is reached.

Make your own judgment about how many twists to work on the edge pairs, and when to add in the extra pairs. Take care to vary the stitches as you work. Remember, this is a lace impression of a leaf, not an exact replica. The aim of all free lace (or any work of art) should be to say something more about its subject than can be achieved in a photograph.

Plate 22.1 *A selection of gum leaves to use as bookmarks or to wear as a brooch (photograph Sue Stafford)*

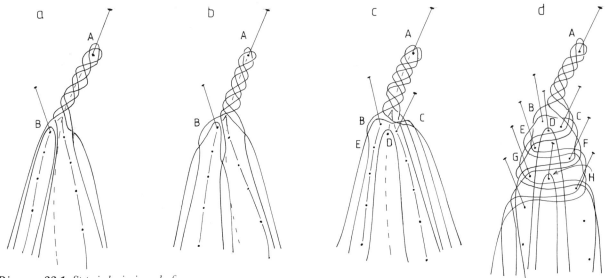

Diagram 22.1 *Steps in beginning a leaf*

Narrow the leaf by spacing the pins further apart, and working in half stitch if necessary. Do not just cut pairs off as this is very noticeable, except in the very finest thread.

The stem

The very simplest way to work the stem is to divide all the threads on the pillow at the base of the leaf into four groups and plait them over the stem outline, using each group of threads as if it were a single thread. Pin through the plait a couple of times to stabilise it. Finish by isolating one thread and using it to bind all the others tightly. It is probably easiest to do this while the leaf is still pinned to the pillow. Secure the end with a collecting knot and remove the lace from the pillow. Hide the end of the binding thread by passing it up into the stem with the aid of a needle. Cut off all the remaining threads at an angle.

Two other ways of making a stem are by cabling, and by working a roll. Both of these are adaptations of traditional techniques which are very useful in contemporary free lace.

Cabling

At the base of the stem separate out the three worker pairs (which will continue the footside edge) and the two edge passive pairs (left and right).

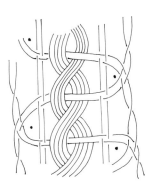

Now divide the remaining passives into two equal groups of threads (usually about five or six threads) and lift the right hand group over the left hand group; this is the first cable twist.

Work the current worker pair through the first passive pair in cloth stitch, then lift them *over* the left hand cable group and *under* the right hand cable group (or reverse the order depending on which side you are working from). Work the last passive pair, then the footside exchange stitch, then the passives again. Now make another cable twist and again pass the workers under the right hand group and over the left hand group. Continue in this way to the end of the stem and finish off as described for the plaited stem (diagram 22.2).

In other situations the cabling technique may be used to narrow a shape gradually by beginning the cabling with less pairs and adding to the groups in successive rows. Then if the shape widens again the pairs may be released.

Working a roll for the stem

Finish working on the left hand side at the base of the leaf. Select just one worker pair and leave the others as passives.

Cloth stitch through all passives from the left then, instead of pinning and working back to the left, simply lift the worker pair back to the left hand side. Pin under the workers and repeat this procedure to the end of the stem, removing the pin and replacing it further along the stem after each row. It is absolutely essential to keep the passives in the correct order, and to tension both passives and workers firmly after each row. You will then see the roll forming. If necessary extra pins can be pushed through the roll after tensioning to assist in following the curve of the stem (diagram 22.3).

This technique can also be used to enclose extra pairs of threads, or even another stem should you wish to make two leaves into a brooch like the one in the plate 22.1.

Finish off as described for the plaited stem.

Diagram 22.2 *Cabling for the stem of the leaf*

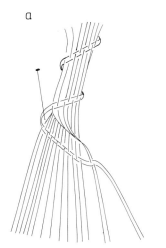

a   b

Diagram 22.3 *Working a roll*

Reading List

Torchon Lace Patterns, Henk Hardeman, Batsford, 1987

Drafting Torchon Lace Patterns, Alexandra Stillwell, Dryad Press, 1986; Batsford 1992

The Torchon Lace Workbook, Bridget Cook, Batsford, 1988

Building Torchon Lace Patterns, Bridget Cook, Batsford, 1992

Pattern Design for Torchon Lace, Jane Atkinson, Batsford, 1987

The Technique of Torchon Lace, Pamela Nottingham, Batsford, 1979, 1993, new edition 1995

The Bobbin Lace Manual, Geraldine Stott, Batsford, 1988

50 New Bobbin Lace Patterns, Clare Burkhard, Batsford, 1993

The Book of Bobbin Lace Stitches, Bridget Cook and Geraldine Stott, Batsford, 1982

Bobbin Lace Making, Pamela Nottingham, Batsford, 1987

Beginning Bobbin Lace, Gilian Dye, Dryad Press, 1986; Batsford, 1995

Russian Lace Making, Bridget Cook, Batsford 1993

Sources of Information

United Kingdom and Ireland

The Lace Guild
The Hollies
53 Audnam
Stourbridge
West Midlands DY8 4AE

The Lacemakers' Circle
49 Wardwick
Derby DE1 1HY

The Lace Society
Linwood
Stratford Road
Oversley
Alcester
Warwickshire BY9 6PG

The British College of Lace
21 Hillmorton Road
Rugby
Warwickshire CV22 5DF

Ring of Tatters
Miss B. Netherwood
269 Oregon Way
Chaddesden
Derby DE21 6UR

UK and Ireland Regional Director
   of International Old Lacers
Ann Keller
Cool Valley
Abingdon Park
Shankill
Dublin
Ireland

USA

International Old Lacers Inc.
124 West Irvington Place
Denver
CO 80223-1539

Lace and Crafts Magazine
3201 East Lakeshore Drive
Tallahassee
FL 32312-2304

France

Centre d'Enseignement à la Dentelle
   du Puy
2 Rue Duguesclin
43000 Le Puy en Velay

Germany

Deutscher Klöppelverband e. V.
Ortolanweg 7
D-1000 Berlin 47

Netherlands

LOKK
Boterbloem 56
NL-7322 GX Apeldoorn

Switzerland

FDS (Fédération de Dentellières
   Suisses)
Evelyne Lütolf
Buhnstrasse 12
CH-8052 Zürich

OIDFA
(International Bobbin and Needle
   Lace Organisation)

UK
OIDFA
Hilary Booth
39 Craigweil Avenue
Radlett
Hertfordshire
WD7 7ET

USA
OIDFA
Kathy Kauffmann
1301 Greenwood
Wilmette
Illinois 60091

Belgium
OIDFA/Belgische Kantorganisatie
Lydia Thiels-Mertens
Jagersberg 1
B-3294 Molenstede-Diest

France
OIDFA
Suzanne Puech
3 Chemin de Parenty
F-69250 Neuville sur Saône

Germany
OIDFA
Uta Ulrich
Papenbergweg 33
D-4930 Detmold

The Netherlands
OIDFA
Puck Smelter-Hoekstra
Corona 68
NL-3204 CM Spijkenisse

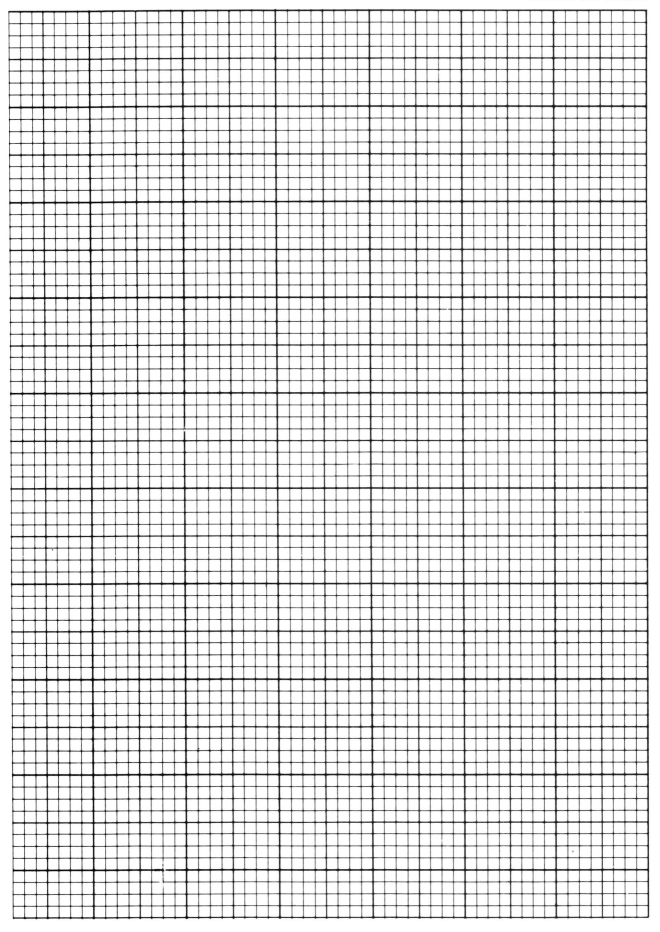

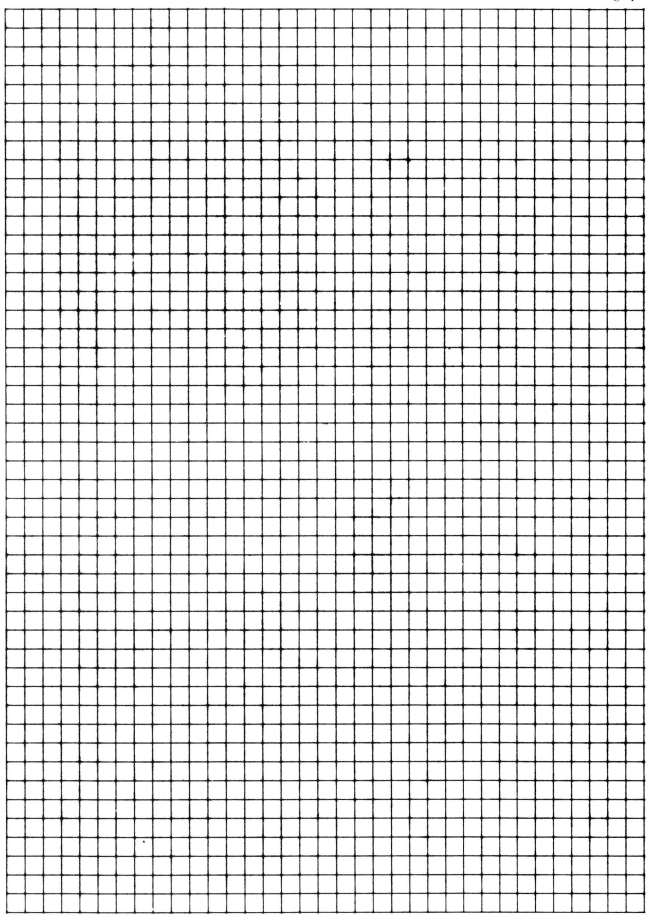

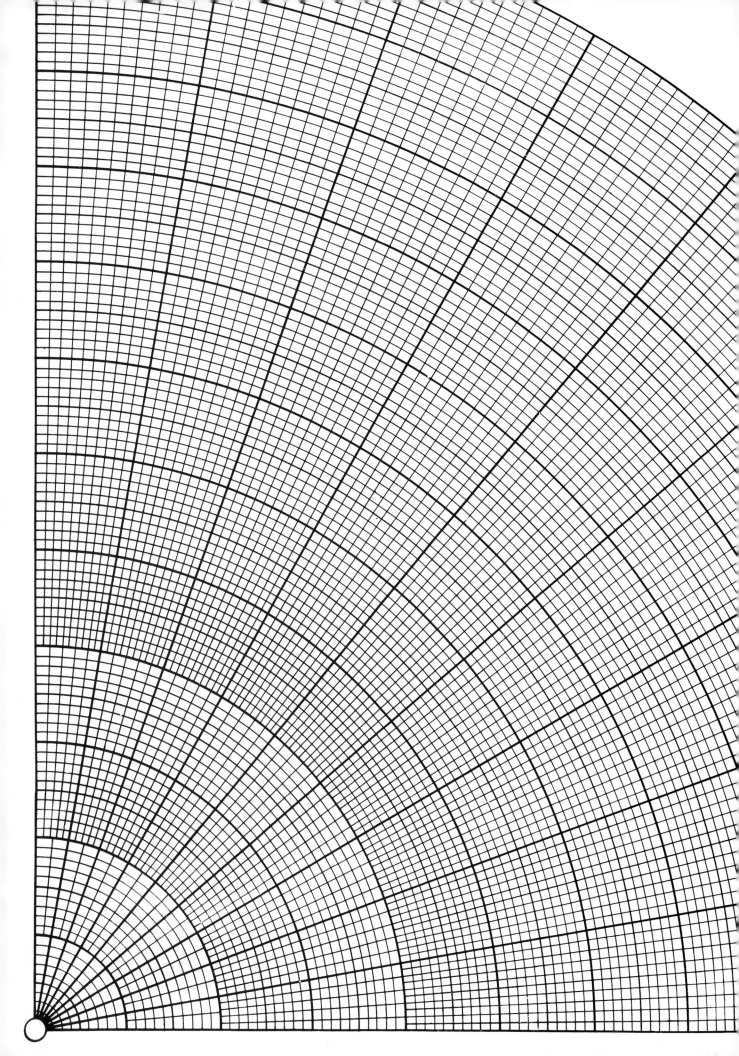

Index